UNDERSTANDING
YOUR
HORSE

WARD LOCK RIDING SCHOOL

UNDERSTANDING YOUR
HORSE

SUSAN McBANE

WARD LOCK

RIDING SCHOOL

WARD LOCK

A WARD LOCK BOOK

First published in the UK 1992
by Ward Lock
(a Cassell imprint)
Villiers House,
41/47 Strand
LONDON
WC2N 5JE

Distributed in the United States
by Sterling Publishing Co., Inc.
387 Park Avenue South, New York, NY 10016-8810

Distributed in Australia
by Capricorn Link (Australia) Pty Ltd
P.O. Box 665, Lane Cove, NSW 2066

British Library Cataloguing in Publication Data

The CIP data for this book is available upon application to the British Library

ISBN 0-7063-6976-9

Typeset by Chapterhouse, The Cloisters, Formby, L37 3PX

Printed and bound in Great Britain by
Mackays of Chatham PLC

Frontispiece. Although horses obviously have to accept human guidance and company and learn to work willingly alone, a regular part of their management should be long hacks in company, even if only with one other animal. This may be difficult with traffic-shy horses in areas where motorised traffic cannot be avoided. If this is the case, perhaps they could be boxed to areas where off-road riding is available. Rides in company with other horses mimic a herd's natural migrations and result in settled, fulfilled animals much easier to work with, and less in need of active discipline.

CONTENTS

CHAPTER 1

NATURE'S HORSE

The horse is one of nature's most specialized animals. It went through many stages in its evolution before reaching the animal we know today. Its evolution is quite well understood and familiar, having one of the clearest and most complete fossil records of the development of a creature from very early times to today. Along the way there were many ancestors and types which, for various reasons, died out.

The animal regarded as the first direct horse ancestor was *hyracotherium* (formerly known as *eohippus*), which was a fox-sized creature with four hooved toes on its front feet and three on the back. It had short, simple and rather weak teeth (compared to today's horse family) and browsed on leaves in the marshy forests where it lived and which covered most of the earth at that time, about 50 million years ago. Most *hyracotherium* fossils have been discovered in America, but a few have also been found in Europe, which is not surprising as the two continents were at one time connected. Land movements and the formation of oceans opened up and closed off migration routes for all creatures, so horse ancestors were able to reach Europe and Asia not only across the Bering land bridge between Alaska and Russia (now the Bering Straits),

but also across the probably extensive wet area that was created as the Atlantic began to form, widen and separate America and Europe.

As the climate of the earth changed, the swampy tropical forests decreased and a new environment – open spaces – appeared with a new vegetation, grass. As its original habitat decreased, *hyracotherium* had to adapt to the new circumstances or perish. Creatures do not adapt consciously to an environment (apart from having the sense to turn their rumps to the wind or shelter in the shade from the sun) nor do they automatically adapt to change. Evolution is not driven by the environment, it follows it. In other words, the fact that plains and grass appeared did not mean that *hyracotherium* would automatically develop the means to cope, in the form of larger, stronger teeth, and longer legs for speed.

Species can only change by means of genetic adaptation. Normally, each parent passes on half the offspring's genes, i.e., the foal receives half its genes from its dam and half from its sire. This heredity is fairly consistent, but sometimes, often for unknown reasons, genes change or mutate, and pass on different characteristics. *Hyracotherium*, with its short legs and relatively poor teeth, was fortunate enough to contain some strains which experienced genetic mutations. Over time these produced descendants with characteristics which enabled them to cope with the changing environment. Over millions of years, creatures developed which had larger bodies, longer legs and necks, longer, bigger heads and bigger, stronger teeth. As the swampy ground no longer played much of a role in the horse's life the number of toes decreased. Very gradually, through several horse-related creatures, the number of toes dwindled to just one – an extreme adaptation to speed and survival in an open, drier environment.

Horses are fast, nervous creatures and these characteristics developed with good reason, for as the horse adapted to its new surroundings, so did animals that considered it good to eat. Predators' hunting skills improved, so the horse's evasion skills had to keep one step ahead if the horse family was to survive.

Although the horse is a specialist running animal, there are creatures on earth faster than the horse, for example some antelopes, and obviously the cheetah which is earth's

A good example of a northern-type equine – stocky body, copious hair to retain body warmth, barrel-shaped body, wide, slightly heavy head, low tail carriage and shortish legs in relation to body size and height. All these are warmth-retaining features. In summer, the change to a much shorter coat is sufficient to make the animal comfortable in a temperate-zone summer.

fastest land animal, able to run for short distances at around 112 km (70 miles) an hour. Large hunting cats peak at roughly the same speed as the horse family – about 48 km (30 miles) an hour. How, then, does the horse family ever get away from a pursuing predator if it does not have the edge in terms of speed? It is known that, in general, predators are successful in only one out of four attempts at a kill, which is not a very high rate; this goes for packs of hunting dogs, hyenas and cats. The horse (or more likely these days, the zebra and wild ass) survives because of his alertness and stamina. If a horse can spot a predator out for a kill while it is still some yards away and can get off to a good start, it can often keep out of reach as it will have attained its top speed within a very few seconds and can keep on running for miles, if necessary, after the predator has had to stop. It is this characteristic which governs much of the horse's nature and behaviour today.

Because it has, for millions of years, had to keep almost constantly on the alert, watching out for danger, this alertness has been 'programmed' into it. Predators do not purposely give warning. Having crept near enough to have a reasonable try at a charge, they spring suddenly, startling their prey; this, not surprisingly, has made the horse family essentially nervous, easily startled and given to galloping off first and stopping to think later. Shying and standing starts are two of their specialities, as most experienced riders will know.

The horse's natural diet also has an important bearing on the needs of the domesticated horse. Grass, leaves and herbs are fibrous foods, even allowing for seasonal fluctuations in moisture and food content, and the nutriment in them is diluted by the fibre and water content. Horses are large animals needing a lot of nutriment, and in order to get the amount they need out of their natural food they have to ingest a lot of it. In natural conditions with a reasonable supply of food, they will eat for about 16 hours a day. Concentrated food is not, by any means, a regular or staple part of the diet of a naturally-living horse, and the equine digestion is not designed to cope with large amounts of grain – which is exactly what so many owners and managers give their horses. Despite about 5,000 years of domestication (which is nothing compared with the 50 million years or so the species took to evolve), the horse's digestive system has not altered appreciably. The domesticated horse is still a herbivore needing large amounts of fibrous food if it is to thrive and feel comfortable, and be mentally settled.

Sleeping patterns in the horse are another give-away to its prey ancestry. Humans, cats, dogs – predators all – sleep for several, indeed many, hours at a time. Perfectly healthy wild and domestic cats, for example, commonly sleep round the clock after a large feed with barely a waking moment. Horses cannot afford to do this. Wild equidae doing so would be rapidly killed off. The horse has developed a system of sleeping for only about four to, at most, six hours out of 24, and in snatches of about 30 minutes rather than all at once at night. Horses sleep at all hours of the day and night. They sleep lightly standing up, locking

Horses sleep and doze lying down, propped on their breastbones, or standing up, but to experience the most restorative kind of sleep they must lie flat out on their sides. In a free herd, or a stabled community of horses, some will always remain standing, even if grazing as well, to keep an eye out for predators (including humans!).

devices in their elbows and stifles enabling them to do so without falling down. This is a particular advantage because they can be off in an instant should danger threaten, whereas it can take several vital seconds for a horse lying prone to be up and off. Horses can also doze and sleep lightly lying down but propped up on their breastbone.

However, they do need to sleep deeply sometimes, and for this they have to lie flat out. This deep sleep, however, lasts for only a few minutes at a time and horses only indulge in it when they feel relaxed, content and secure – one reason why newcomers to a yard are often found not to lie down for some days or weeks, depending on how quickly they settle

in. In the wild, depending on the size of the herd, there are always sentries standing up ready to warn the herd of danger, and if you go down any line of boxes in a yard late at night you will find some horses are lying down and one or two are always standing up. As a horse gets up one of the sentries will lie down and take his turn asleep. This sleep system also means that horses need to have some food available during the night to keep them naturally occupied and replete, yet in almost any domesticated yard the hay ration is finished by midnight or before, leaving the horses with a long, unnatural period without food until first feed, something which would never happen in the wild.

The horse's senses are much more

This Arab is a perfect example of an equine which evolved in hot, dry regions of the world. Even in winter his coat is short and fine. His body is slender with long legs and high tail carriage for air circulation around the buttocks, and his head is shorter, finer and lighter than his northern cousins.

acute than ours and he can hear sounds higher and lower and at much longer distances than we can. His sense of taste is acute, as is the accompanying sense of smell, and these account for horses being such fastidious feeders, turning down food which looks and smells quite all right to us. The horse's eyesight is different in many ways from ours, and this vital sense has a chapter of its own (Chapter 3). Because of his super-senses and, many believe, extra sense often described as 'extra-sensory perception' for want of a better expression, horses often behave in ways we cannot explain or understand, and the less 'thinking'

horsemen and women may often unjustly punish a horse who is behaving as his evolution, instincts and senses tell him to, because they can see no immediate reason for his behaviour. This, of course, hardly makes for a harmonious relationship between horse and rider!

DIFFERENT HORSE AND PONY TYPES

The earth has a much more varied climate than in the days of *hyracotherium*. As the earth's climate changed over millions of years, those species genetically able to change with it survived and developed physical characteristics suiting them to the area in which they lived. Horses and ponies from cold regions have thicker skins, woollier winter coats, slit-like nostrils to keep out excessive amounts of cold air, and shorter legs related to their barrel (body) size than those from hot areas. Their need is to retain body warmth for most of the year. Their tail carriage is lower to prevent too much heat escaping from between the buttocks. The blood vessels carrying warm blood are not so near the surface of the skin so the heat cannot radiate out so easily, and their bodies are rounder so as to preserve an inner core of heat more easily. Their mane and tail hair is often profuse, wiry and even wavy, in order to trap more warm air close to the body. The neck, for instance, is thin and heat can easily escape from it, so long, bushy mane hair, often on both sides of the neck, helps retain body warmth.

On the other hand, breeds and types evolving in hotter regions look quite different. They have thinner skin so that the blood can lose heat more easily, their nostrils flare easily to let out hot air, the body coat, even in winter, is shorter and finer as is the mane and tail hair. The tail carriage permits body warmth to escape particularly during and after action when this is most necessary, and the legs are longer, permitting greater air movement round the more oval-shaped body, both of which characteristics promote the loss of body heat. In addition, they often have shorter heads for their size than animals from colder climes, which need longer air passages, and a longer head, for cold air to travel up warming it to a comfortable temperature,

before arriving in the lungs.

Both types of equid, however, have an average body temperature of about 38°C (100·5°F). The commonly used terms in the horse world of 'cold-blooded' and 'hot-blooded' types have no basis in fact, neither are they an infallible guide to temperament ('hot-headedness'). Although one may reasonably guess that a Thoroughbred, for instance, may be more nervous than a cart-horse, this is by no means always the case.

Man has mingled the natural horse and pony types to such an extent that there is probably no truly wild, untouched type left. Even the

Another feature of horses from hot regions of the world – blood vessels prominent under a thin skin. These are close to the surface, so that the heat in the blood can easily radiate out to the surrounding air helping to cool the body.

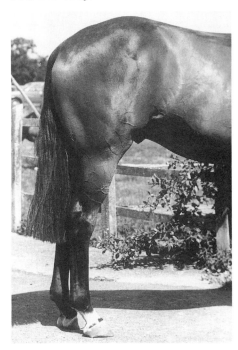

Przewalski horse, which is a different species from our domesticated horse and has a different number of chromosomes (hereditary structures), now has its breeding controlled by man and can no longer be called truly wild. The term 'feral' is used to indicate free-living animals which have in some way been interfered with by man or which have domesticated ancestors. Examples are Britain's native ponies, the Camargue horses of southern France, America's mustangs and Australia's brumbies. The re-introduced Przewalski herds in Askania Nova in the Soviet Union are now feral – but it would be nice to be able to believe the very occasional reports which appear of sightings of true, wild Przewalskis in places like Mongolia and Sin Kiang province in China. Unfortunately, wild horses now seem to have the same status as the Yeti.

By keeping alert, horses detect possible danger. This Welsh Mountain Pony shows the alert head posture, using three of the five senses used to detect danger – ears pricked to pick up sound, in this case from the front, eyes on the sides of the head to give almost all-round vision, and nostrils flared into a circle to pick up scents that may help identify the nature of the danger.

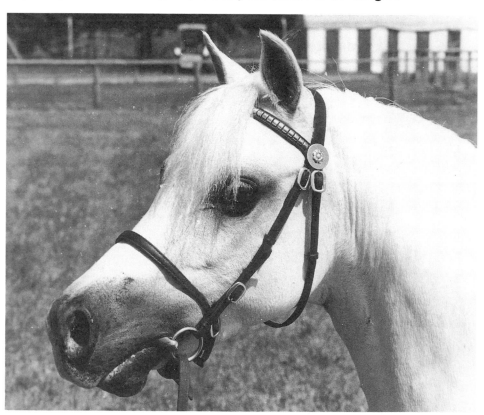

COLOUR

Horses' physical characteristics, enable them to cope with widely differing climatic conditions, but where does colour come into it? Domesticated horses come in a wide range of colours and markings and, as in the case of Palominos, can almost be produced in any colour within the range with reasonable reliability. But colour was originally evolved for camouflage. The most common colour, from the evidence of cave drawings and paintings, and the descriptions of ancient historians who were familiar with truly wild horse herds, was a sort of dun/beige/light brown range, and this colour would certainly blend perfectly with the tundra and parched plains of the northern regions and Asia.

Many scientists feel that *hyracotherium* was probably mottled and/or striped, as are many forest animals, to disguise it in the dappled light filtering down through the trees. Zebra striping on legs and eel stripes down backs are still seen on some animals, particularly those of pony ancestry or breeding. The dapples in the coats of some greys, browns and bays, and a few chestnuts, are presumably a remnant of prehistoric mottling.

Zebras seem, at first sight, to be positively calling attention to themselves, but seen against the brush and long grass of the savannah they are, in fact, superbly camouflaged.

As always, man took advantage of genetic mutations as far as colour was concerned, and as new, strange colours appeared he learned to breed for colour, and often still does, although, as with blood temperature, it has no bearing on the horse's temperament. Chestnuts are not 'hot-headed' or fiery, blacks are not weak and cowardly, greys are not necessarily lacking in stamina, and browns and bays are no more dependable than horses of other colours (but see Chapter 4 for information on ways in which colour can affect management).

CHAPTER 2

THE HORSE'S MIND

Opinions vary as to how intelligent horses and ponies are, or whether most of their actions and reactions depend on instinct. It is widely stated that horses have no reasoning power, but many experienced horsemen and women will refute this. The power of reasoned thought indicates a fairly high level of intelligence in any animal and is said to reach its zenith in the human race, although arguably dolphins and their relatives show a higher level of intelligence, reasoning and 'civilized' behaviour than many humans. But where does this leave the horse? If reasoning power is, as defined in the dictionary, the ability to think through cause and effect, the power to solve problems by thinking about them, then horses do certainly possess reasoning power. Also, it should be remembered that humans think like predators (ask any competent businessman!) whereas horses think, and reason, like prey. It's not surprising, therefore, that they should think and reason in a way different from humans.

The measure of intelligence in evolution, apart from genetic heredity, is how well a creature survives *in its own environment* given the body it has and the surroundings in which it finds itself and to which it has adapted. As horses have survived down to the present day they must be clever at avoiding adversity and protecting themselves and their young. In their own environment, mainly grassy plains and shrubby regions, they survive supremely well. More surprising, however, is that as a species, the domesticated horse has survived in an environment designed and regulated by humans, to the extent that there are many millions of horses living and working with and for man. This shows a high degree of *mental* adaptability and consequent intelligence; mental because there certainly has not been time during 5,000 years of domestication for the horse's physical workings to adapt to the highly artificial management systems and surroundings which most domesticated horses have to tolerate. Yet the horse is sufficiently mentally agile to learn what is wanted of him, and to realize that if he does such-and-such a thing he will be praised even if only by winning his handler's approval. Sadly, some horses have such brutal handlers, all they learn is that by doing such-and-such a thing they will simply be spared a beating or some other physical abuse such as being pulled in the mouth or jabbed by spurs.

Another point of view is that horses must be stupid or they would not allow themselves to be ridden, driven and generally dominated, however

Horses are 'programmed' by evolution to want and need movement. In the wild, *equidae* are on the move for much of each 24-hour day. They become over-stressed and frustrated if not given enough exercise. Whether escaping danger or letting off steam, horses can go from standing start to full-speed gallop in less than five seconds. They bring their hind legs under them and lower their quarters, like this, to give thrusting power, the head and neck are raised to lighten the forehand and facilitate forward impetus and the ears, eyes and nostrils are on 'red alert', to pick up information from the environment.

mildly. It should be remembered that this submission to control is not natural to them; it is the result of long training, brain-washing if you like, usually from extreme youth. Would anyone deny that humans are trained and 'brain-washed' into accepting the rules and regulations of the society in which they live? Yet this is not regarded as stupid behaviour on the part of humans.

Horses are *not* stupid; they are extremely sensitive and intelligent beings. Where humans often go wrong is in trying to test equines' intelligence by scientifically-devised tests which attempt to gauge their intelligence (normally their problem-solving abilities and, therefore, their reasoning power) and measure it in comparison to human intelligence. This is like giving someone who has learned only French at school an examination paper in German and expecting them to be able to do it.

Horses and ponies like socialising not only with their own kind but with other animals – even humans! Domesticated horses are easier to handle, more settled and content when allowed to take part in the daily life of their establishment, and get to know and mix with other residents.

A free-living wild or feral herd of horses or their relatives will have a stallion, a lead mare, young and older females and other males up to about a year or 18 months old. At this age they become sexually mature and are expelled from the herd by the stallion. They join bachelor bands until they, in turn, can fight for and take over a herd.

PRIORITIES

As herbivores with voluminous intestines which are meant to be at least half full most of the time, the horse's main preoccupation is food. When threatening situations arise, such as an attack from some other creature, food is temporarily forgotten and the urge for self-preservation surfaces. Horses think at such times of getting away from danger. Other thoughts are occupied with self-comforting actions such as rolling and scratching, sheltering, socializing (extremely reassuring to a herd animal like the horse) or letting off steam. Breeding animals, at the right time of year such as spring, summer and autumn, if the climate is warm,

obviously think about the physical satisfaction of breeding and mating.

Many trainers claim that horses think about their work and that this is why they improve in training. What is more likely, however, is that training activities are stored in the sub-conscious. Then, when asked for a particular movement in the future, the horse is better able to produce it because the sub-conscious part of the brain has mastered it.

HERD HIERARCHIES

Horses are like humans, and many other creatures, in that they live by strictly-defined social rules and hierarchies, with dominant herd animals (usually mares with one single

17

Stallions fight to keep their herds or to gain control of one. Usually, they will not fight to the death but they can seriously injure each other. At some point, it becomes obvious to one that he is not going to win, and he will retreat.

'elder' mare as the real boss), in-betweens and doormats. Under this system peace normally reigns and each animal knows its place. The stallion seems on the surface to be the boss and he does herd up his mares and chivvy them about but only for his own purpose – that of keeping them together in his harem in order that it is his genes that are passed on to the next generation, not those of some usurper stallion. The really important decisions in a herd, such as when to move to fresh pastures or shelter, where to go and at what pace are normally decided by the lead mare. Even mating is ultimately dictated by the females, for in horse society this only takes place when the mares feel ready, not when the stallion wants. The mares are supremely

indifferent to which stallion is in residence at any particular time: their genes will be passed on anyway.

In domesticity, herds even exist in a yard of stabled animals. Friendships form and enemies develop. Some individuals are naturally more dominant than others. There is no doubt that horses are under more stress in an unsettled yard with a floating population such as a livery yard, a competition yard or, especially, a dealer's yard, than in an establishment which has the same horses nearly all the time.

In the wild, any strange horse trying to enter a herd will be subject to kicking, biting and rejection by the established members until, by testing out the individuals, the newcomer finds out where on the social rung, the 'kicking' order, he or she belongs. It is quite wrong for a newcomer to a yard, or domesticated 'herd' of horses at grass, to be bundled straight out with them in a paddock without any introductions as this is likely to result in him being quite seriously injured or, at best, ignored and spurned by the others, which will be as upsetting to him as being alone. Horses, being herd animals, do need company and need to feel they belong.

The right way to introduce newcomers is to stable them next to a low-ranking animal in the herd, to ride out with him and perhaps lead them about in hand together. Then put them together, with *no* other animals, in a paddock to cement their friendship. Gradually, over several days, the other horses can be brought in, the low-ranking ones first. If possible, it's a good idea to have the two, temporarily separated, herds in neighbouring fields with secure, safe fencing, so that the new horse can at least see and perhaps smell and touch the others over the fence and get to know them without risk of injury. Some experts will maintain that this is asking for trouble, but in my experience it works well. There will be some squealing and chivvying around however careful you are, but the gradual method will not only be more likely to keep your horse physically safe and sound, but will also enable him to make friends and be accepted, which will not happen if he is simply pushed into an existing herd like the

It is essential for foals to have lots of freedom and other foals to play with if they are to grow up both mentally balanced and physically well developed. Foals should have an outdoor life with plenty of shelter. During their first winter if they have Arab or Thoroughbred blood in them they should come in at night.

Thinking of three things at once. This horse is taking note of the direction in which his handler is leading him, and following willingly; he is also paying close attention to the photographer with one ear pricked towards the camera, and his other ear is flicking to his right where he is noting something taking place out of the picture.

intruder they will consider him to be.

When stabling is being arranged, there is absolutely nothing to be gained by putting two enemies next to or even near each other. Horses should be carefully studied to ensure that they really do like their neighbours. If there is any kicking of walls, restlessness, bad faces, loss of appetite or a general air of discontent, move one or both and find more congenial neighbours.

Riding out is also important. It is unreasonable to expect all horses to agree with all others. It will not teach them a lesson in discipline to try to

force them to hack along peaceably together. Any sensible horse person will keep enemies separate and allow friends to work together. Of course, if a friendship is so firm that the two will not work individually this can create problems, but the two should be allowed to be together in stables and paddock. They should not be separated permanently, as some experts advise. They can be trained, by strong but sympathetic riders, to realize that when work is on the cards they must take their cues from the humans involved. Once the lesson is learned there will be no more trouble.

WHAT DOES YOUR HORSE THINK OF YOU?

You have probably never really considered this. Humans obviously have to take the place, during work and general handling, of the horse-leader in a natural herd, but this does not mean that humans should try to bully or dominate the horse by harsh physical means unless the horse itself is doing the same to the human. Safety of both human and horse is most important, and an undisciplined horse is a danger to itself and everyone near it. Horses with strong personalities and dominant inclinations are best left to experts to deal with, when a mutually respectful partnership may be formed. Novice riders should work with and ride only well-trained animals, who submit willingly to human wishes, until they have more experience.

Horses do soon spot humans they can boss around, and many will 'try it on' to see just how far a particular human will let them go. This especially seems to happen with young horses who, once they reach the stage of having mastered basic training and are feeling stronger, fitter and more confident with their roles, frequently try a little rebellion to see just what the score is. Horses easily spot bullies (who are essentially cowards at heart), weaklings (whom they may boss), beginners (with whom they may often be helpful and sympathetic, believe it or not), professionals (which means they can often have a buck and a kick without fear of unseating the rider), vets (needles!), farriers (variable!) and non-horsey people who pat them on the head as if they were dogs.

The best attitude to adopt when around horses is one of quiet confidence. Horses are not mind-readers: they judge you by your aura and the impression you create. Cultivate your acting skills if you are unsure of yourself, but don't go too far the other way and bustle brashly and noisily about as horses resent this. Calmness, firmness and understanding are what are needed, and if you are genuinely having trouble with a horse call in a sympathetic expert before letting matters go too far, because once a horse has won a battle with you he

Attention full ahead. With his head up and ears and eyes all directed forwards, this horse is alert and interested, but quite calm as his half-closed nostrils indicate. This clearly shows the horse's eyes on the sides of his head not the front.

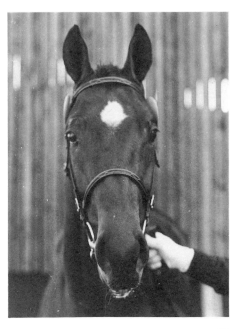

Dogs chasing horses in a field exactly mimics what happens in the wild when, say, wild dogs hunt zebras in Africa. Horses may panic, and may blindly gallop into trees and buildings and kill or injure themselves. Some horses, however, may keep their heads and kick out in defence, seriously injuring the dogs. Unless you are very sure of your horses' and dogs' behaviour, it's best to keep dogs on a lead when near horses.

will remember that he once got the better of you, and his opinion of you will never be quite the same again.

THE COMMON CHARACTERISTIC – NERVOUSNESS

You may find it rather strange that horses in general may be described as nervous, especially when you think of courageous police horses going where angels would fear to tread, patent-safety children's ponies, or elderly schoolmaster cobs, but the fact is that underneath the veneer of domestication and training, plus

experience of the human race, horses *are* nervous because their evolution has programmed them to be so.

Horses have survived over millions of years by being constantly on the alert for danger, and this has made them essentially nervous. It is another reason for cultivating a calm, confident attitude when around horses. Sudden movements and sudden noises frighten them. They react first and do so like lightning. This reaction will usually involve head up/hind legs under/muscles taut, which is the exact mode which enables them to gallop away at an instant's notice. Unfortunately, when they do so they do not think about the proximity of any humans, dogs, other horses, wheelbarrows, cars (moving or stationary) or anything else which may be in their way and this is how accidents happen, both to the horse himself and to other objects, living or inanimate.

It is important to get the horse to associate a particular sound from you, such as 'whoa' or 'easy', as meaning everything is all right and you are in control, there to protect him and nothing is going to hurt him. It is worse than useless to shout at the horse, to reprimand him for being alarmed and, worst of all, hit him. He will associate being shouted at, told off and having pain inflicted with whatever alarmed him as this is how his mind works, and this will just make him much worse next time so that eventually, instead of becoming a calm, trusting, reliable animal as his training progresses he will develop into a defensive, dangerous, maybe even aggressive, nervous wreck.

It is not easy to keep your head, especially when cornered in a loose box by a panicking horse, and there are times when your own safety must be paramount, but generally if you can make it your second nature to control your reactions and to come out automatically with calming words you will have much more success in handling and dealing with horses. Self-control is vital, and a calm lead from you can quell most nervous reactions from horses.

MEMORY

Horses and ponies have excellent, clear and extremely long memories. This is another characteristic which has helped them to survive. They not only had to remember the location of water-holes and the choicest grazing areas over many square miles of territory (sometimes hundreds of square miles), but also where predators habitually lurk, where competitive horse herds may be, and where shelter may be found.

Horses remember each other for many years and show reactions at meeting each other again after long gaps. It seems probable that they also remember humans but do not always show it as much. They remember places and routes particularly well, even if they have only experienced them once and especially if something particularly memorable (good or bad) happened to them in that place or on that road. This is why a horse, once having shied at a particular spot on a lane, will probably shy there for ever more, expecting whatever alarmed him first time round to jump out at him again. This is why it can often be so difficult to re-train horses out of bad habits or past teaching. Patience and consistent aids and vocal commands can eventually override old habits, but they may resurface in moments of stress or lack of concentration. Get the horse used to 'no' as his only reprimand in such cases, and reward him profusely for learning anew.

CHAPTER 3

THE HORSE'S EYESIGHT

Like all his other characteristics, the horse's eyesight is ideal for a plains-dwelling prey animal. He has an almost all-round field of vision as he needs to be able to spot predators wherever they may be. His eyes are set to the sides of the head, whereas most prey animals' eyes (cats, dogs, humans) are at the front where their attention is normally directed. The horse's pupils have a horizontal oval shape and the field of vision is correspondingly wide and panoramic. His legs are fairly thin compared to the bulk and weight of his body, and his head quite long. Therefore, when the horse has his head down grazing, his eyes are several centimetres above the ground and he can see almost all round (except for directly behind him) between his legs, which offer little obstruction to his sight. Even the area behind him can be covered by a slight turn of the head. The neck is quite long to enable the teeth to reach the ground and this also means that by swinging his head round the horse can, again, easily see right behind him, whereas humans have to turn round if they want to see clearly behind them.

Everyone is familiar with the experience of spotting something 'out of the corner of their eye', and they then usually turn their heads so as to look at it with both eyes and get a clear view. This use of two eyes is called 'binocular' vision. The horse, however, uses one eye only to look at most things: called 'monocular' vision. Where the two eyes' fields of vision cross over directly in front of the horse, he does have binocular

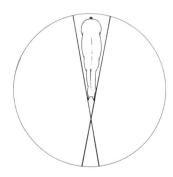

Because the horse's eyes are on the side of his head he can see all around his sides apart from just behind him. He sees most clearly in front of him but no closer than three or four feet, where he can use and focus both eyes.

Doing what comes naturally. Whether in the wild or in a paddock, grazing horses can see virtually all round them; and can cover the whole 360° area by a slight turn of the head, their comparatively thin legs offer little obstruction to their vision of approaching danger – such as humans wanting to catch them.

vision. Monocular vision enables the horse to see much more, but results in poor depth perception and a flat view, making it difficult for him to judge, for example, just how far away a predator or other object is. Even when the horse uses binocular vision, for example when galloping headlong away from something startling such as a lion, lorry or piece of paper blowing in the road, not to mention a marauding dog, he may not see clearly where he is going.

In order to focus on objects, the horse has to move his head into different positions. This directs rays of light through the lens of the eye on to various sections of the retina at the back of the eye, which then transmits

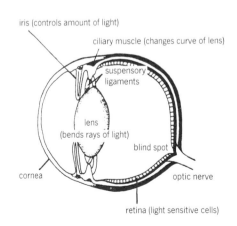

Cross-section of a horse's eye.

the picture to the brain. In humans, the lens is quite flexible and changes shape readily to focus on different objects. Unless we have a vision defect, we do not need to wave our heads up and down or round about to focus on something. The horse does, however, because his lens is less flexible. To see things in the near distance he must raise his head and bring in his muzzle in the 'collected' position. To see objects that are very close, he must actually move his muzzle and look at them mainly with one eye, because his muzzle gets in the way. To focus on objects in the far distance, he raises his head but does not need to tuck in his muzzle.

For a galloping horse whose head must move up and down and backwards and forwards in accordance with his gait, this motion constantly interferes with his focus on what lies ahead and at least partially explains why galloping equidae (for this applies to donkeys and zebras, too) not infrequently gallop headlong into objects which can kill them, such as trees and brick walls. This is one reason why it is so imperative to try to stop a bolting horse, because he cannot be trusted to steer clear of obstructions in his path. It is not

A horse's eye, set on the side of his head, enables him to see almost that entire side without moving his head. This horse is clearly looking at something behind him and to his left. His head is facing forwards but his eye is turned to the back, so he can clearly see what it is.

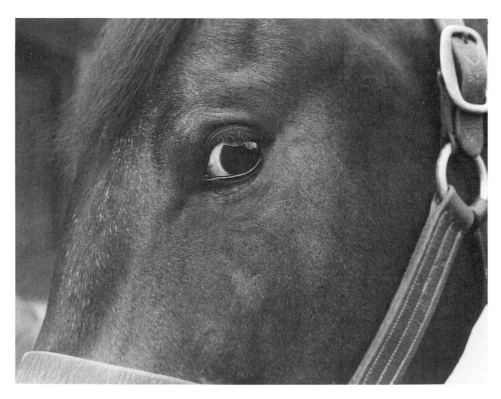

advisable to 'let him run himself out' as is sometimes recommended. Another reason for the horse's apparently poor vision when galloping is that he may actually be short-sighted, as some experts believe.

One old theory which has been disproved by recent research is the horse's inability to pick out colour. It was believed by some that horses are colour blind, but it is now known that they have similar colour-discerning cells in their retinas to humans, and can probably pick out red, orange and yellow quite well, and also green, but may have difficulty with blue and violet. There have been many stories about horses being startled by seeing riders in red coats when first introduced to the hunting field and many very experienced horsemen always denied the old theory about colour blindness. If, as used to be supposed (and doubtless still is by some), the horse really did see things in shades of grey, it is unlikely that he would react with surprise and apprehension at just one particular shade of grey (depicting red). Some horses may well be colour blind, just as some humans and other animals are. However, this does not prove that all horses are by nature colour blind.

It is often said with some admiration that as the horse cannot see well directly in front of him – indeed, probably cannot see at all directly in front of him for a distance of about 1·2 m (4 ft) because of the side placement of the eyes – it is nothing short of a miracle that he can jump fences. However, this is not particularly marvellous as human athletes function in the same way. The time-lapse between judging the fence and losing sight of it as one actually takes off (whether you are equine or human) is so short that it does not make a lot of difference. No human jumper keeps his eye on the rail all the time he is jumping.

COPING WITH EQUINE VISION

An understanding of the horse's vision affects the way he is schooled, ridden and handled.

First let us discuss 'gadgets' – riding accessories such as the different reins and martingales available to help the rider not only control the horse, but 'encourage' him into an acceptable outline. Probably the main point to realize is that in order to focus on, and therefore see clearly, where he is going the horse needs to be able to move his head quite freely. This is necessary for the rays of light to be thrown, as described, on to the correct part of the retina for clear discernment. It is clear, therefore, that *any* item which restricts the horse's free use of his head is automatically restricting his vision. By preventing the horse from using his head, and therefore his eyes, as nature intended a rider is in practice partially blinding him. No wonder so many horses are unnerved by or fight for their heads against tight standing martingales, harsh bit contact, forced outlines, side-reins during lungeing and so on. In addition to the fact that, as a prey animal, the horse naturally fears constraint (enough on its own to panic some horses), he is being deprived, at least partially, of his most valuable sense, his sight.

Much time should be spent in building up a young horse's

The horse must be given freedom of head and neck if he is to focus clearly on the fence and so have a chance of jumping it safely. It is quite possible to do this and keep a light, communicating contact on the bit.

confidence in his human handlers and trainers before expecting him to conform to their training ideals. Horses can be and are schooled to do all sorts of movements, from a very collected canter and one-time flying changes to jumping high, wide fences at racing speed, but they need time to develop trust in humans as so many of the things asked of them, from collected outlines to performing at speed, require the horse to work with restricted vision. Probably the most natural competitive sport is endurance riding, in which horses are given more or less complete freedom of head and neck and allowed to measure their own paces, so that their bodies are working as nature designed. Apart from slowly building up muscles and sinews, not to mention heart, lungs and digestive system, in order to perform the work asked of him, the horse has to be accustomed gradually to working in a way he probably would not choose, left to himself.

I do not wish to alarm readers or exaggerate our effects on the horse, but it is an aspect of management and training which seems to be little considered and perhaps more thought could be given to it. It is certainly one very good reason for always using the voice when working around horses (not allowed in dressage tests but essential when driving), so as to warn the horse we are present and of what we want him to do. Sudden movements certainly frighten horses unless they are well and truly conditioned to human handling and know that nothing is going to hurt them. However, instinctive reactions may take over at any time, so it is wise to remember that horses can see widely if not, perhaps, sharply or with good depth perception, and that this can easily account for them shying at, say, a piece of paper in the hedge, because they possibly cannot tell that it is a harmless piece of paper without looking at it more discerningly.

Because of his almost all-round

vision, the horse can also see a good deal of you when you are riding him. He can certainly see your legs, whip and, if they are carried slightly out to the side, elbows and hands. It is not clear if he can see well from your shoulder level upwards, but if you can see the corner of your horse's eye when, say, riding on a circle, it is likely that he can see you, too. For this reason, many expert trainers, when backing a youngster, ask their helper not to sit up when first actually sitting on (rather than lying over) the horse's back. If the helper leans down, chest on withers, the horse will not be alarmed by the sudden appearance of a human high above and behind him. A sitting appearance and posture can gradually be taken up over a few days, accompanied by much reassurance and praise from the trainer on the ground.

When a horse is being lunged, his speed can be considerably influenced by the position of your body. If you take up a position opposite his hip, you seem to the horse to be rather behind him and urging him on. A position opposite his shoulder or head has the effect of slowing him down as the horse perceives you to be coming in front of him. The whip is meant to reinforce our body position: by holding it towards the tail the horse may be urged on whether or not you flick it, and by pointing it in front of him he will soon learn to slow down or stop. Well-trained circus liberty horses rarely take their inside eye off their trainer, whose body position and whip movements they note as their cue for different movements. Famous circus trainer Mary Chipperfield once said that her horses could do their act on their own just by listening to the music and following that, and all she had to do was position herself and her whip correctly to get them to stop.

When a horse is first backed the rider should lean down on the horse's neck so he will not be frightened by someone suddenly appearing above him.

When schooling jumping horses, it is obviously sensible to use as many different shapes, depths and colours of fences for an all-round education as is possible. If the horse gets used to all colours, even those he cannot see too clearly, and types of fences, he will be less easily fazed in the ring when the time comes. It is also a good idea to keep fences freshly painted, as the reflection of light (sunlight or floodlights) off the newly painted fences usually used in formal competitions can very easily frighten and confuse horses if they are not used to it. They do, however, have in-built 'sunglasses' in the form of the *corpora nigra*, little dark brown 'lumps', for want of a better word, above the pupil, which are believed to shade them from excessive sun and assist vision during a life in the open.

Horses sometimes go, or are born, blind and remarkable stories have been told of how well they can continue to live an apparently satisfactory life. One televised display of jumping by a blind horse was achieved by a person standing by each fence and clapping or blowing a whistle while the rider verbally counted the horse down and over the jump. Another horse was known to me who was completely blind but trusted his rider implicitly. She placed his forefeet on a board immediately outside his box so he knew where he was and to step up slightly to enter.

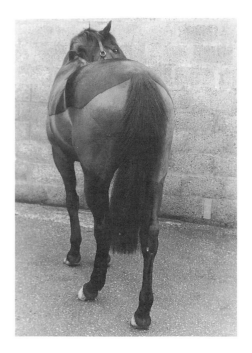

Although the photographer is standing behind and to the left of this horse, the horse simply has to turn his head slightly to the right and turn his right eye to the back for a clear view of what he may be doing, without moving a leg. To do this, humans would have to turn right round; so would a cat and most dogs.

Inside, his hay and water were always present and always in the same places. She hunted him for years before he was ultimately put down at home due to a heart defect. So it shows that with understanding, empathy and commonsense, even lack of this most vital sense can be overcome.

CHAPTER 4

THE HORSE'S SKIN AND COAT

The horse's coat is one of the most reliable indicators of his condition and inner health. Any disorder will show to some extent in the coat, and this includes mental disorders such as being discontented, over-stressed, unsettled perhaps due to having changed homes, bereavement (which covers not only mare and foal being separated at weaning, when both suffer bereavement, but also a friend leaving the yard permanently), and so on. Feeding problems are quick to show in the coat, particularly malnutrition or a meagre diet with vitamin and mineral deficiencies and, the classic problems internal and external parasite infestation.

The skin and coat form a remarkable protective layer almost all round the horse, the hooves being the only areas not covered. At the natural body openings the skin runs continuously into the mucous membranes inside the anus, vagina, sheath, lips, nostrils and eyes. Skin, hair and horn are, in fact, different versions of the same substance, all being made mainly of a hardened protein substance called keratin. If one is unhealthy the other two will be out of sorts, too. Their health and condition is almost entirely dependent on diet. A good, balanced diet in accordance with the horse's needs will produce healthy skin, hair and horn unless there is some disease present.

Skin is elastic, has a natural tension strongest in the young, and a complicated structure allowing for many functions. It is composed of two main layers, an outer, dead layer called the epidermis and a sensitive under-layer, the dermis. The epidermis is made up of cells which are always dying off and being replaced by live cells from the dermis. The dead cells flake off and can be seen as the dandruff in an ungroomed horse's coat.

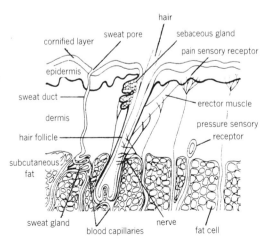

Cross-section of the horse's skin.

The dermis contains the nerve endings which enable the horse to feel pain, pressure, pleasure, irritation, heat and cold. There are tiny blood vessels called capillaries in the dermis which form a mesh of routes for the blood carrying food and oxygen to all parts of the body and carrying away the waste products formed by processing food and just by living. The skin's blood supply also helps regulate the horse's body temperature. Blood vessels expand in order to transport more heat-carrying blood, so excess heat can radiate out through the skin. When the horse is cold, however, these vessels contract, they then carry less blood and thus help conserve heat.

Also in the dermis are the oil and sweat glands. The oil (sebum) is a natural lubricant which helps keep the skin moist and pliable. As it is secreted out of the hair roots or follicles, it is spread over the coat and skin, helping to protect it from excessive moisture and other possible injurious substances. It also protects to some extent against friction. Grooming helps distribute the sebum over the skin and coat, and body brushing removes excess amounts which build up in a stabled horse shielded from the weather.

Colour originally evolved as camouflage and to either deflect or attract the sun's rays according to the climate. The interesting dappling on this pony would make excellent camouflage in the mottled light and shade of a forest, an environment in which the earliest horse ancestors evolved. A woolly winter coat indicates that this pony's ancestors had a northern origin.

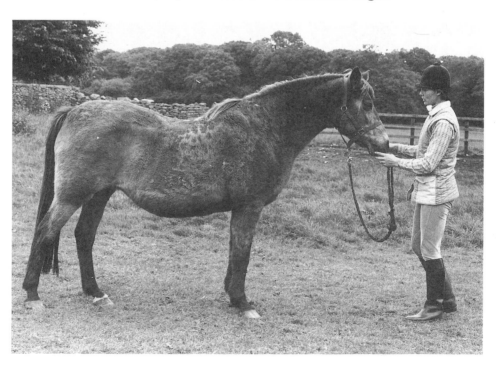

All members of the horse family are basically herd animals and normally feel much more secure and content with others around them.

Above: Scratching a horse gently on the withers is a sign of friendship in horse language. The ultimate compliment is for him to try and scratch you, too, with his teeth!

Opposite: It is pleasant to be able to deal with your horse outdoors in good weather provided he will stand quietly tied. This horse is tied to a string loop which will break should he become startled and pull back hard enough. The author would prefer the post to be used rather than the rail, which may also break. Opinions vary on whether tying a loop like this is a good idea, as once a horse has learned that he can break free he may always try it. However, with a mature and therefore extremely strong horse, it may not be possible to cure him of the habit. In the long run, it may be safer to allow him to break free into an enclosed yard than to struggle with his immense strength and risk injuring both himself and his handlers.

Left: Daily damp-sponging of eyes, nostrils, lips, sheath or udder and dock is important to keep the skin clean and comfortable and is very refreshing to the horse.

Right: The coat hair does not grow all in one direction but often has whorls in it. This fan-shape occurs at the hip. The coat direction has evolved to facilitate the drainage of water from the body. The siting of circular whorls and other hair patterns can be used to identify individual horses.

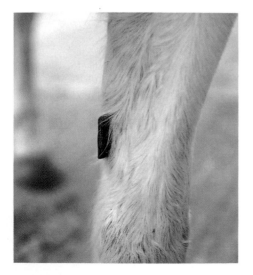

Left: These horny patches inside the pony's legs, above the knee and below the hock, sometimes grow too long and if they do not flake off naturally and cannot be easily picked off by hand, the farrier should be asked to trim them when shoeing. Each horse or pony's chestnuts, as these patches are called, are uniquely shaped for him, as individual as a human's fingerprints, and by photographing them you have a helpful record of his identity should he be stolen.

Right: Thinking of two things at once! This horse has one ear on the photographer and one flicking back to pay attention to something to the side of or behind him.

Left: Horses get their sleep in short snatches around the clock: they can doze and sleep lightly standing up.

Right: The horse's eye is set to the side of his head, so by a slight turn of the head he can see all round him.

Above: Walk quietly up to the horse or pony, possibly offering a titbit in your out-stretched hand. Most horses will wander up to see what you've got.

Left: Although a good, strong and safe manger, this is rather too high to enable the pony to feed comfortably.

Above: Don't give titbits like this as the pony might accidentally grab your fingers. Always give titbits on a flat hand with your thumb also down at the side, not in your palm where it could be mistaken for food!

Right: Horses who terrorize their handlers at feed time can be discouraged by a strong squirt of water in their faces from a plant sprayer, or water pistol.

Above: When feeding loose horses together, stay to see fair play. Ideally place the containers about 16 feet apart.

Below: Doing what comes naturally. Horses were meant to eat for about 16 hours out of 24. Their digestions only work optimally when fed according to this regime. Hay or hayage, and roots, substitute grazing for stabled horses. Hydroponic grass can also be used.

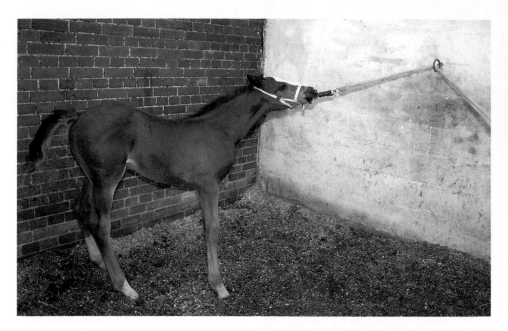

Above: The most effective time to teach a horse to submit to handling is when young. There are various methods to teach a foal to be tied up but this is one of the most effective and safe. The foal wears a well-fitting, strong headcollar or slip and has a long rope or lungeing rein fitted to it, passed freely through a ring in the wall and held by a handler (out of the picture). The foal can be 'played' on the rein by the handler so he is not unduly frightened by a rigid, fixed feeling. The handler talks to him, teaching him the command 'stand' or 'whoa'.

Left: Even worse than keeping a horse stabled is preventing him from having a sense of freedom, of sorts, by caging him in like this. An intelligent creature can soon resort to neurosis such as stable vices, not to mention being made thoroughly miserable, by this treatment.

Above: When turning out a horse or pony, before letting him go make him stand still for a few seconds while you pretend to adjust his mane, or something similar, so he doesn't get into the habit of charging off when *he* feels like it.

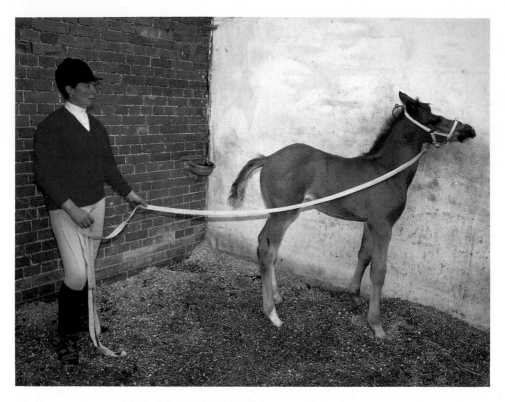

Above: Foal roped for the first time. The foal has realized that he is not going to be hurt and that, in any case, he cannot get free, and is standing quietly. He will not forget this lesson.

Opposite, above: Vary your horse's exercise. A lesson can be interesting for the horse or very stressful depending on how it is carried out. A half-hour intensive lesson is also quite tiring and should not be carried out until the horse is at least half fit, say six weeks into a fitness programme from being completely soft.

Opposite, below: The horse loses sight of the jump on take-off and jumps a 'memory'. So that he can judge his landing, freedom of head and neck are essential.

Right: Boredom is anathema to horses. This expression shows unhappiness and stress.

Above: Most horses want and need company. Solitary ones spend much time moping by the fence or gate, often looking yearningly out at civilization, the stable yard, a distant field with animals in it, or even humans, to appease their loneliness. Some may resort to jumping out, with the risk of injury to themselves and others, plus damage to property.

Above: Insufficient exercise can make many animals prone to playing up or being generally difficult. Exercise, whether ridden or at liberty, should be regarded as a priority far above sweeping the yard or tidying the tack room. Horses were meant to be on the move most of the time and domestic horses and ponies nearly all suffer from lack of gentle, natural exercise.

Above: Rearing is extremely dangerous and very hard to cure. It can be caused by a painful mouth, rough handling of the bit or a very dominant, unwilling temperament. Spirited horses may do it if really exasperated with their riders, or a horse may rear if something suddenly startles it, or is simply trying to get the better of the rider. This rider is doing the right thing by sitting still so as not to unbalance the horse, and holding on to the mane and leaning forward to stay in the saddle. As soon as the horse lands she should make him move on and keep him moving as he cannot rear unless he first stands still.

A healthy skin produces a healthy, glossy coat: together they comprise an elastic, resilient envelope covering almost the whole animal, protecting the horse from the outside environment, helping regulate his vital body temperature, excreting toxins in the sweat and carrying nerve endings which inform him about his surroundings.

The sweat glands are active most of the time although you do not normally notice sweat on a horse unless he has been working hard or the weather is very hot, because it usually evaporates away before making the horse noticeably wet. Sweat carries away with it some of the waste products mentioned earlier, and also body heat, which evaporates from the body with the moisture. This is another cooling-down mechanism.

Another important substance, melanin, is located in the dermis, and this gives the skin and hair their colour. It has a strengthening effect on the skin, too; and although colour does not affect temperament it can affect the way a horse is managed, and also resistance to irritants such as weather and flies. Within reason, the more melanin present in the skin the stronger, or better protected, it is. Black, brown and bay horses would seem to have most melanin, but grey horses also usually have dark skin under their coats. Chestnut and palomino horses have least and can, as many know, be more susceptible to weather and flies.

White markings, those on the face and limbs, normally have pink skin under them, which indicates a complete lack of melanin. Such areas are certainly more prone to diseases like mud fever and rain scald, and more likely to suffer from photosensitivity (sensitivity to light or the sun's rays). Horses with large areas of white hair on pink skin, such as piebalds and skewbalds, may be very prone to rain scald and mud fever (which is not confined to the legs but can affect the belly, too, an area often lacking in colour in such horses). It is sensible to keep a special eye on them and make sure they always have access to shelter if they seem to succumb to these disorders. The old practice was to let mud dry and then brush it off, but most veterinary surgeons now advocate rinsing off mud with clear water and then drying the horse very thoroughly afterwards. Brushing can certainly minutely scratch the skin by rubbing the mud grains into and along it, and this makes for easier entry by the mud fever germs. It is the thorough drying after rinsing which is vital, and horses who seem to have rather dry skin can be helped by an emollient cream such as E·45 or others on the market or available from a vet, or by the use of a little liquid paraffin (not heater paraffin) rubbed into the skin. Unfortunately, this is slightly oily (which is why it protects) and will need washing off with soap from time to time before another application.

Skin thickness varies with the area of the body; it is thickest over the top of the neck, back, loins and quarters and thinnest in areas such as the legs (particularly along the insides), belly and the muzzle, the most sensitive area of all, which the horse uses as his

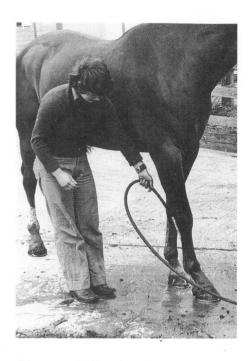

Rinse mud off rather than let it dry and brush it off afterwards, as this often scratches the skin and favours the development of mud fever, a painful and troublesome skin disease. Skin and hair should be thoroughly dried after rinsing, perhaps with a hand-held hairdryer initially, then by stable bandages over padding or pieces of old mesh blanket. A supply of old terry towels kept in the yard is also useful for initial drying off.

equivalent to our fingers, investigating just about everything with it. Cold-blooded breeds such as Shires and other heavy horses, native ponies and horses from northern lands have the thickest skin overall, and those originating in hot climates the thinnest. The latter also tend to sweat more. In general, thicker skin is found where the horse needs most protection from the weather, and thinner skin where he needs less protection but increased sensitivity.

The skin does, of course, possess the capacity to heal itself when damaged, and even really serious wounds may, in time, heal with scar tissue (which is not as strong, sensitive or flexible as the original). Wounds can become infected, however, and should the infection get into the bloodstream the horse may become seriously ill and die. However, the horse's immune system may be able to cope if the horse is healthy. In domestication, of course, problems are normally put right long before this stage is reached by cleaning and treating wounds correctly and promptly. It should be remembered, however, that infection can enter a wound as it occurs, so even a few hours delay can give the germs a head start. For this reason, clean and treat all wounds as soon as they are noticed. And don't leave grass-kept horses for days, or even one full 24-hour period, without checking on them for this reason, as well as for security and general health and well-being.

The purpose of the coat hair is to help protect the skin and regulate body temperature. Hair itself is hollow, and the layer of hair over the skin traps between its individual hairs a layer of body-warmed air right next to the skin. Air is a poor conductor of heat so this helps greatly to keep the horse warm in winter, when, depending on his breeding, the horse may grow a long, thick coat. The longer the hairs, the more they overlap and the more air is trapped. In summer, the need to keep warm is less urgent so the coat is shorter.

Skin, hair and horn are closely 'related' – if one is unhealthy the other two may be. The quality of them all stems from a correctly balanced diet. Here the feet are grossly neglected, broken and cracked; a condition exacerbated by poor health and diet.

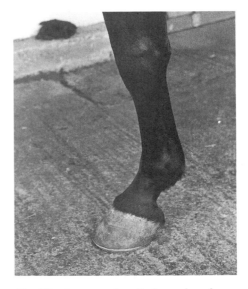

Healthy horn and well shaped and shod feet. Farriers are not miracle workers and cannot be expected to keep shoes on feet with poor horn.

Hair grows in swathes over the body, not straight down all over it, and this is especially to direct the rainwater to drainage routes which show up when the horse is wet. When the horse is wet, the warm-air layer is destroyed so heat escapes from the body much more quickly and effectively. This means that if the horse is wet with rain, he can become chilled whatever the time of year if the weather is cold. If a wet horse is kept standing around, even if initially over-warm, he will cool down quicker than his coat dries. Still being wet, heat will continue to escape from his body and he will become too cold. Wet horses in chilly weather should be kept walking or gently trotting about under saddle or in hand to prevent this. Grass-kept horses must be watched to see how they are responding. Contrary to general opinion, long periods of rain bother them, and they may stop grazing when sheltering or simply because they are preoccupied with feeling cold and miserable. This, in turn, cuts down their energy intake, energy they need to create body warmth, and they lose condition and become less resistant to the chill – and so it goes on. Proper shelter must be available, preferably in the form of an ample field shed, or more than one if there are a lot of horses out, to ensure that all have a chance to shelter and are not kept out by bullies or dominant horses. This will also help prevent the development of exposure ailments like mud fever and rain scald. Trees are insufficient shelter as, during prolonged or heavy rain, water accumulates and falls on the backs of the sheltering horses in larger drops than normal.

The coat hair is cast (shed) over several weeks in spring and autumn and a new coat grows, suitable for the season.

Many horses are clipped during the autumn to reduce the heavy coat during work in winter. It is not possible for a horse to work hard and stay in condition, or even comfortable, if he has a normal winter coat, unless it is of the exceptionally fine variety produced by some Thoroughbred horses. Nearly all working horses need clipping to some extent at least in winter, and the variety of clips will be familiar to readers. It is also well known that coat clipped off to enable the horse to work without undue sweating, loss of condition and subsequent chilling must be compensated for when he is not working by means of clothing.

Most horses' winter coats are fully set by the end of November or earlier, and if you can wait until this time you should be able to get away with only one clipping. If you clip earlier some coat will regrow, leaving the horse less bare. Some yards insist on clipping every fortnight or so while the coat is still growing to keep the horses smart, but there is really no need for this. It is inadvisable to clip much after New Year as the summer coat will start to come through in late winter and clipping will spoil it.

The coat grows at least partially in response to the weather, responding to hormones secreted by the horse's brain which are triggered off by light and temperature. Coat change is all part of the horse's normal biorhythms or body clock: shortening days and lowering temperatures result in the onset of the winter coat production;

Working horses usually need clipping in winter to prevent excessive sweating and subsequent chilling. However, there is nothing to be gained by removing too much coat. This is an Irish clip in which the hair is left on the whole of the quarters and hind legs. A variation is the 'chaser clip' – popular for steeplechasers – where hair is also removed from around the tops of the hind legs. These two clips are quite adequate for most working horses in winter. They leave the top part of the horse protected while removing the hair from those areas which sweat most.

The head hair is removed for smartness, although in horses who object to this scissors or hand clippers can be used to smarten up the under-jaw area and ears; the horse will probably allow his head to be done with hand clippers.

in late winter the reverse is the case, lengthening days having most effect on the summer coat assisted by later increasing temperatures. This ties in with the breeding season, although in the Thoroughbred industry foals are expected to be born as near 1st January as possible. Commercial breeders often provide extra light, clothing and warmth in the stables to fool the horses' brains into thinking spring is just around the corner, and this not only brings them into summer coat much earlier but into breeding condition by setting off their sexual cycles as well.

You can control your horse's coat to some extent without spending money on heat and light. If you don't want to clip, or your horse is bad to clip and you don't want to drug him to do so, simply start rugging him up at night from late August onwards, increasing his clothing (while still remembering not to overload him and make him hot and uncomfortable) as the weather gets cooler. You will find he grows a much shorter than normal winter coat. Similarly, don't be in too much of a hurry to reduce clothing in later winter and spring, and you will find he loses his winter coat earlier, too. However, if you then remove his clothing altogether and the weather becomes unseasonally chilly, you could find he produces a rather longer summer coat than you would like.

The mane and tail hair also help protect the horse. For horses kept out in winter, it is much kinder to leave their tails full, plaiting them up for special occasions. Pulled tails result in considerable heat loss from between the buttocks, an area of thin skin, especially as horses naturally shelter from wind and rain by turning their tails to it. However, if you really like pulled tails, a turnout rug with a tail flap should be used in winter. It costs money to keep weight on cold horses, so be kind to your bank balance and your horse by not overdoing the hair removal. Most people clip much more extensively than is really needed, most 'ordinary' working horses managing very well with a blanket clip at most.

Horses naturally stand with their tails to the weather to protect their sensitive heads. The thin skin between the buttocks is an area where body heat is easily lost. If horses are kept out a good deal do not pull (trim) the tops of their tails or they lose the protection they need.

Hair which should never be removed is that on the muzzle, for these are no ordinary hairs but whiskers with a copious supply of nerves around their roots. They are used as antennae, helping the horse sort out his food, assess objects with his muzzle, and preventing him bumping into things in the dark, as do the whiskers around his eyes. Unfortunately, many people, particularly in the showing and hunting disciplines, feel a horse looks smarter without these important antennae and think nothing about clipping them off. Even an unclipped horse can look very neat if he is neatly trimmed with long hair under the jaw removed, and hair protruding from the edges of the ears especially at the base, fetlock hair trimmed and manes and tails tidied.

Although a horse left to itself will be rained on, blown about, will roll in the mud (which in fact cleans away excess grease and discourages skin parasites), and scratch himself on any convenient rubbing post he can find, thus keeping his skin and coat in perfectly healthy order, most people want their horses cleaner than nature allows. Stabled horses must be body-brushed to keep down the protective grease and dandruff which is not removed from them by natural means. Grass-kept ones should have this left in the coat, although a light body-brushing before a special occasion will certainly do no harm.

At one time it was regarded almost as a crime to wash a horse, at least in civilian stables, although it always seems to have been the practice in military ones. When washing a horse ensure that he is properly dried afterwards, as exposure of wet skin to cold breezes or even cold air, causes the skin to crack and chap.

Shampooing with soap or even special animal shampoos can be overdone. In some stables it seems to have reached the stage where, instead of relying on the natural deep gloss that results from good health, proper management and good grooming, commercial coat dressings are used to sleek up the dried out, dull, over-soft coats caused by the removal of virtually all the natural oils in the animal's coat. Rinsing down with clear water removes some grease, and soap of any kind is not really needed unless the animal's coat is excessively greasy, or badly stained with manure or urine. It is also better to use slightly warm water than cold, and this can be achieved by fitting to the yard tap the sort of instant water-heater used on some domestic showers, which heats water as you use it. Set the thermostat at the temperature of the horse's body – about 38°C (100·5°F) – and this will do fine for winter and summer.

Electric groomers are a great boon to busy owners. The vacuum-cum-rotary brush type is the most practical, removing most dirt and sucking it into a bag rather than sending it out into the atmosphere to land on and be breathed in by everyone, human and equine, in the vicinity. A good session once or twice a week with one of these will save a lot of time and energy on other days and, together with the occasional rinse down, will keep the horse clean enough for anyone's standards without denuding him of his natural protective lubricants.

CHAPTER 5

THOUGHTS ON FEEDING

Feeding is probably the one item in a horse's management which affects him more than any other. Others are very important, of course, particularly freedom and exercise, but feeding is something which occupies a horse's mind most of his waking hours. It is obvious that too little food can result in poor condition or even death, and too much will cause obesity, laminitis, colic and so on, but the quality of a horse's diet is as important as how much he is given.

Novice horse-owners are greatly helped today by the many good prepared diets on the market. Cubes have been around for some time, but many horses and ponies fed on just cubes and hay do become very bored with their food and go off it. The new coarse mixes (called sweet feeds in the USA) have been widely available for a few years in the UK and Ireland and it has been found that horses seem to prefer them to cubes, and can be given the same coarse mix plus hay or a hay substitute indefinitely and are still keen to eat.

Both cubes and coarse mixes, if of a reputable brand, will be specially formulated to suit horses and ponies of given categories. There are mixes for hard-working horses, those in light work, those on box rest who simply need enough nutrients to keep them ticking over perhaps following convalescence, those who are sick and so on. As well as having the correct amounts of energy, protein and fibre (bulk or roughage), these products will also be properly balanced as regards vitamins, minerals and trace elements.

It is a common and potentially serious mistake to add vitamin and mineral supplements to prepared, branded feeds such as cubes or coarse mixes as this will probably result in unbalancing the diet, which can cause all sorts of disorders in the horse. Another mistake is to feed cubes or coarse mixes along with other 'straight' (single) ingredients such as oats, bran, barley, flaked maize and so on, for the same reason.

Prepared feeds have an analysis on the bag stating what they contain as regards protein, fats (oils or lipids), energy (carbohydrates, which are starches or sugars), fibre (roughage), vitamins, minerals and trace elements. Even if you do not understand the significance of the analysis – and few owners, even experienced ones, do – you can get your vet or a nutritionist to explain it and give an opinion as to whether this particular product is suitable for your horse and the work he is doing. You very rarely get an analysis with straight feeds: you may have an idea from looking at, smelling, handling and tasting the feed, whether or not it is of good quality but not of what it actually offers as regards food value. The only way you can be sure of this is to get it analysed by a laboratory, which your vet could arrange if required. Bear in mind, however, that you would have to do this for every single new batch, sack even, of feed if you really wanted to know what the feed contained.

For novice owners in particular, a branded coarse mix is recommended, used in accordance with the maker's instructions. This will give you a measure of control over what nutrients your horse eats, unless you can properly analyse straight feeds.

Hay, too, is a large and vital part of your horse's diet and this, too, should be analysed – easier as it is usually purchased in larger amounts and sometimes has an analysis. Horses eating a hayage product because of respiratory problems or simply because their owners want them to be on a healthy, 'clean air' regime, will find the analysis on the bag or polythene sack containing the product, and can again ask for expert advice on its suitability. This analysis should be looked at against the concentrate analysis (that for the coarse mix or cubes). The two together, forming the major portion of the diet except when the horse is at grass for long periods, can be adjusted to give the horse an ideal diet which not only provides his nutrients but also leaves him satisfied and not looking for more.

NATURAL FEEDING METHODS

As already described, horses and ponies in natural conditions or out at

Horses originally lived in forests browsing leaves from trees and shrubbery. They later evolved to eat grass.

grass will spend about 16 hours out of 24 eating, during both day and night. Contrast this with the sort of diet regime most domesticated horses are on and you will see that feeding management is often well out of kilter with what nature requires for the horse.

The horse's food is digested by means of enzymes (chemicals) in his digestive juices, secreted all along the digestive tract starting with saliva in the mouth, and by bacteria (also called gut micro-organisms or gut flora). The bacteria are alive, and need a more or less constant supply of food – the horse's food – if they are to remain healthy and do their work.

If there is a long gap in the horse's intake of food (such as during the night, or when the horse is out at some event for the day) these bacteria are known to start dying off. This obviously means they are not available to process the next lot of food which comes along and the horse can, as a result, develop colic (which is indigestion, mild or severe). In nature, this almost never happens. Truly wild animals can migrate to other feeding grounds when the grazing in one region fails, but domesticated horses on a bare paddock in summer can also suffer. The digestive system does, to some extent, shut down and retain some of its contents when food has not been forthcoming for a few hours, but the many hours often inflicted upon domesticated horses without any food available cannot be tolerated by the gut bacteria and they fail.

Another vital point is that certain bacteria process certain kinds of feed. As they do best on a fairly regular supply, it is best to feed your horse the same ingredients in each feed, varying only the amounts of each according to the horse's workload. For example, do not feed cubes for breakfast, coarse mix for lunch, straights for tea and something else for supper. Once you have worked out the daily amounts of each ingredient in your horse's diet, put some of each into each feed (even whatever roots you choose such as carrots or soaked sugar beet pulp) so that your horse's digestion is not upset by the constant change. One of the well-known golden rules of feeding is to make no sudden change.

On the subject of sudden changes, there is another still-common practice which is most unhelpful to a horse's digestive system, and that is giving a weekly mash (usually bran) the night before a day off. True, the horse's concentrate ration must be severely reduced (but not removed) along with his lessened workload, but a bran mash is not the way to do it. Many established texts state that the horse must have a 'laxative diet' before a rest day. Why? If the horse is constipated there is probably something more seriously wrong with him than one bran mash can put right. If he is not constipated, why does he need a laxative?

An excellent low-energy feed suitable for a resting horse can be made up by mixing grass meal and soaked sugar beet pulp, provided these ingredients are part of the horse's normal diet anyway. So that the bacteria still get their supplies of concentrate feeds, however, do include in it a single handful of whatever concentrate mixture the horse normally has. Another low-energy feed might consist of, say,

Concentrated feeds, such as coarse mixes, cubes (nuts), barley, chop and so on are best stored in vermin-proof, galvanised metal bins like this, which usually have a fastening to prevent horses gaining access, gorging themselves and making themselves ill! Never tip a new load of feed on top of existing supplies but use up the old batch before cleaning out the compartment and tipping in the new delivery. However, keep back some of the old batch to mix up the new for a week or so, to enable the horses digestive system to get used to the slight change. This applies even with the same type of feed.

molassed chop (often wrongly called chaff, chaff really being the outside husk of milled grain) with roots or soaked sugar beet pulp, again with a single handful of concentrates and provided these ingredients are normally given to the horse, even if only in small amounts.

Another reason for not feeding a bran mash is that bran is a very unbalanced feed as regards two important minerals – calcium and phosphorus. Horses should have more calcium in their diet than phosphorus, the current recommended levels being 1·5 parts calcium to 1 part phosphorus, whereas bran is very high in phosphorus and low in calcium, and produces a sudden change in diet. In addition, a continually unbalanced feed of this type (as can result if owners mix a lot of bran with their horse's feed thinking that it simply bulks it up) results in bone disease. Bran is expensive, tasteless and hard to digest, which is why it has a laxative effect.

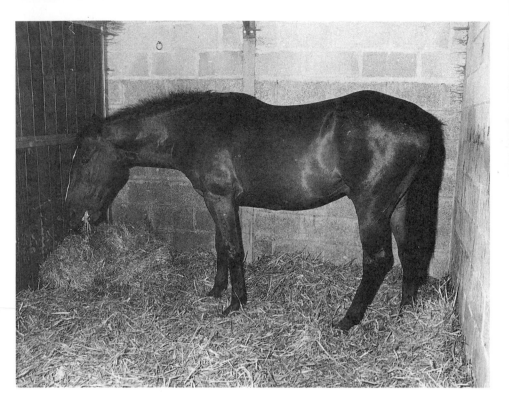

Giving a horse or pony a more-or-less constant supply of hay or similar roughage imitates nature by keeping the digestive system gently occupied most of the time. Most people feed too many concentrates and not enough hay. Feeding from the floor, like this, is quite acceptable, except with a horse who flings hay all over the place. It is the standard method in top-class studs where foals and other young-stock may get caught up in haynets, hayracks or other hay holders.

The horse can easily do without it.

Probably the easiest and most effective way of following nature's rules as far as feeding is concerned is to see that the horse has a more or less constant supply of hay or hayage except for an hour or two before work. Horses at grass will be adequately catered for in this regard, and can actually be ridden straight off grass, without allowing time for the grass to 'go down', provided the work is slow for at least the first half hour and preferably longer. Horses at grass, like those with water constantly available, do not wolf down their feed like hungry horses fed mostly concentrates, but 'trickle feed' as nature intended, taking in their food little and often. Horses with a fairly constant supply of roughage do the same, and can safely be walked and gently trotted. If the horse is going to be doing more strenuous work, however, it's safest to remove his hay supply two hours before work, or at least one hour depending on the type of work. It is, however, quite wrong to deprive even the hardest-working eventer, racehorse, hunter or whatever of his hay and water for several hours, as is commonly done. This does his digestion and his mental state, not to mention his metabolic energy supply so vital for work, no good at all.

Large, occasional feeds are contrary to nature and do not encourage good digestion. The horse's concentrate ration or his ration of 'false' (non-concentrate) feeds such as chop and roots should be split into three or more feeds a day. In any case, 1·8 kg (4 lbs) per feed (not counting hay or hayage) is enough for the horse to cope with at one meal. It is a good plan to give his largest feed at night so that he has more time to eat and digest it, and in cold weather it will also provide more warmth during the night, although sustained consumption of hay is better for this.

For horses who are very good doers, needing little feed to keep condition, owners may be worried that even hay may make them too fat. If you get an analysis of the hay or hayage you are considering, simply make sure that it is of a lower energy grade than usual. The hayage manufacturers can give full details of a suitable grade for such animals. Also, feed it in their special small-mesh nets so the horse has to wheedle out a little at a time and so spin out his ration over a longer period.

GRASS

Grass, leaves and herbs, plus roots and grain in smaller quantities according to season, are the horse family's natural food. In their natural environment horses have a wide variety of plants to choose from and will instinctively balance their diet. Research into grazing preferences has shown that horses naturally select a wide variety of grasses, wandering about from area to area, and showing individual preferences for certain foods above others.

In domesticated paddocks, horses may find that their selection of grasses is very restricted. Most paddocks and fields are sown with a predominantly ryegrass mixture. Matters are improving, however, with more species being included in seed mixtures plus herbs, although the latter usually have to be specially requested by the owner.

Both soil and herbage analyses need to be carried out to discover what nutrients are available to grazing horses: once this is known, steps can be taken to improve the pasture according to the category of animal to be grazed on it – breeding stock, working performance horses, 'everyday' riding horses, cobs, ponies and so on. Many horse paddocks are extremely neglected and provide little more than an exercise area, but from the point of view of providing the horses with a fairly natural, varied and balanced diet, and of saving money, well-tended pasture is an important part of horse management, for it is certainly much cheaper than buying in other feeds.

Generally, grass is at its most nutritious, with its highest protein content, in spring (if it is not over-grazed). During the summer the grass coarsens and its feed value wanes.

45

A 'horse-sick' (over-grazed) paddock will have areas of extremely short grass and areas of longer, rank (tough and sour) grass with droppings in them. These are the 'lavatory' areas and are ignored by the horses for grazing unless desperate for food. A field in this condition is useless for feeding value and will contain parasite larvae which will infect the horses.

Then there is an autumn flush of growth which has more energy value than summer grass. In winter its food value is negligible, except in a mild winter when it may go on providing a moderate level of nutriment. Grass, however, cannot be grazed all year round without being ruined. It must be treated (probably harrowed and fertilized) and rested on a rota basis if it is to remain healthy and productive. Fertilizer firms or specialist equine nutritionists can advise on suitable grassland care for horses and ponies.

WATERING

Most horses have water always with them in either the stable or field and this is by far the safest and most satisfactory way of providing them with water. Wild horses will trek to water-holes night and morning, if near enough, although it has been noted that zebras frequently go for four days or so between drinks if their grazing grounds are a long way from a water-hole. Left to themselves, feral horses and those in domestic paddocks will drink frequently in small amounts during a 24-hour period.

One of the rules of feeding states that horses should be watered before feeding, and in the days when they were only watered two or three times a day this was correct as a long draught of water after a feed would certainly interfere with digestion. The comparatively small amounts a horse may drink during and after eating when he has water always with him do no harm. In fact, it is now believed that this practice actually aids digestion. The water must be clean, otherwise the horse may keep himself short of water, which can have a very bad effect on his health.

If, for some reason, you cannot leave water always with your horse, he must be taken to water (or vice versa) at least twice a day – certainly first thing in the morning and again before the evening feed. It is a good plan to offer water again after work and during the late night check. Give the horse plenty of time to drink. Horses will usually take a long drink then lift their heads and rest for a minute or so.

Then they will usually drink again. Don't make the mistake of dragging the horse away during that rest as he will then go short of water. Let him take his time and drink his fill. It is safest to let the horse himself move away from the water when he has had enough. It is an important process both for the horse's peace of mind and his physical health, so do let him decide when he has had enough, unless he is being rationed for some reason, or is hot and tired from work. In the latter case he should be allowed small amounts every quarter of an hour or so (no more than half a bucket) until he is cool and rested.

During long hacks or endurance rides, horses should be allowed to drink en route, particularly in hot weather, to prevent dehydration.

Friendly horses will drink out of the same container with no trouble. Horses may take a drink, then raise their heads to rest, like the horse in the foreground on the right, before having another drink. When watering horses in hand at a trough, do not pull them away before they have had their second drink. They will usually move away of their own accord when their thirst is quenched.

CHAPTER 6

HANDLING

Horses and ponies are big, strong creatures easily startled and quick to panic. Their minds are such that when frightened they think of only one thing – self-preservation. It is very hard to get through to a frightened horse and often strong measures have to be employed, but not, however, painful ones which will make the horse even more convinced that there is something around to be afraid of. Correct handling means safe and effective handling. It aims to get the horse to do what you want without him being afraid. In this frame of mind he will learn that he will not be hurt, and will not be asked to do anything which he finds painful or distressing. In other words, mutual trust and confidence are developed.

There are odd exceptions to this state of affairs, of course. For example, vets do sometimes have to do things which may be very unpleasant and occasionally painful, which is why horses quickly recognize them. Vets probably have a distinctive smell about them which horses associate with members of their profession and which we cannot detect, because many horses retreat to the back of the box with a worried look on their faces at the approach of a vet, even one whom they haven't met before. The same goes for farriers. If a horse has been mishandled by a farrier, roughly

treated, hurt or frightened, it is often a long time before that horse will trust other farriers. He may easily start on the slippery slope of becoming bad to shoe. Vets and farriers are trained in the handling of difficult horses, and in methods of restraint not recommended to be employed by non-expert members of the public. If a horse has ever been subjected to this kind of control he will remember how worrying it can be and cannot be expected to understand that it is for his own good.

There are right and wrong ways to do everything, and often more than one right way. The methods of handling recommended in this chapter have been tried and tested over the years and are all effective and safe to use with well-mannered animals. The techniques described are basic ones everyone working around horses needs to know.

LEADING IN HAND

It is essential that your horse becomes used to being led from both sides, not only the left as was the old teaching. Horses led from only one side can become notoriously difficult about being handled on the other side and this can be dangerous. Saddles and bridles invariably fasten up on the near (left) side as do throat-latches but

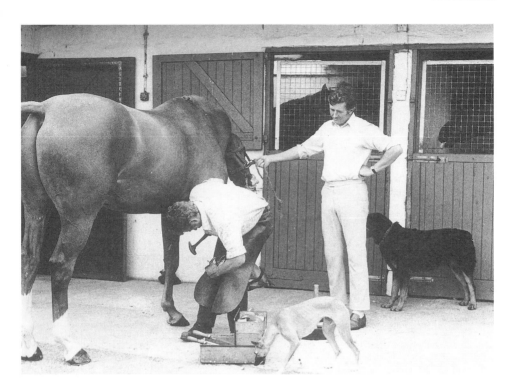

It is often better to hold a horse, if someone can be spared, rather than tying him up. This makes it easier to calm him should he object to something slightly unpleasant and uncomfortable, like being shod. If a tied horse pulls back in fear, he can either break free or frighten himself even more as he realises he is firmly restricted. The dog in the foreground is after a piece of hoof horn which dogs often like to chew and eat!

there is a lot to be said for girthing up on the off (right) side as often as the near. All riders should be equally adept at mounting and dismounting from the off side as the near.

To lead in hand from a headcollar, position yourself at the horse's shoulder, not in front of him where he can easily knock you over with a thrust of his head (accidental or otherwise) or tread on your heels. It is usually recommended that when leading horses you wear your hard

hat, gloves and strong boots or shoes. This should certainly be the case on a public highway, but it is impractical for leading around the yard and turning into paddocks. Strong shoes, however, should be worn, not trainers, and ideally not wellingtons, although most people wear the latter for everyday stable work.

Hold the lead-rope with the hand nearest the horse about 15 to 30 cm (6–12 in) from where it is clipped to the back ring of the headcollar under the horse's jaw. Hold up the spare end with your other hand so it does not trail dangerously on the ground, where it could be trodden on by you or the horse and result in one of you being tripped up or brought down. Never wrap the rope round your hand or wrist as, should the horse suddenly be startled and take off, you could be dragged along and badly injured.

The horse should understand some command such as 'walk on' from his lungeing days, or even just a click of the tongue, so give the command and walk with him, staying at his shoulder. To stop, simply say in a slightly long-drawn-out tone, 'whoa' and perhaps pull slightly on the rope. To turn him, always walk on the outside of the bend so you are, in thought if not fact, pushing him away from you. If you pull him round towards you there is more likelihood of his treading on you and becoming unbalanced, as he will follow you rather than make his own way round the curve. Tie a knot in the end of the rope to help stop it being pulled through your hands.

To lead from a bridle, bring the reins over the horse's head and use them as a rope, but remember that your contact is now directly with the horse's mouth so treat it gently. Hold the reins together as for a rope. If the horse is also saddled, loosen the girth a hole or two but not so much that it might cause the saddle to slip round under the horse's belly, and run the stirrups up their leathers so they do not swing around, bump into the horse or catch on things. It's a general rule, 'rider off, stirrups up'.

Leading on a road is something most people have to do at some time. It is always safest to lead on the road in a bridle, or at least a lungeing caveson with the leadrope clipped to the front ring on the noseband. Both these methods give more control than a headcollar. It is unlawful to ride or

When leading a horse or pony on the road, keep well to the left and walk on his off (right) side. Wear a hard hat, gloves and strong shoes or boots and carry in your right hand a long schooling whip to give you control of his quarters should he play up.

Top. How *not* to lead a horse. Never get in front of the horse like this, as it is very easy for the horse to tread on your heels and cause an accident and injury, or push you over with his head.

Bottom. This is the right way to lead. Stay by the horse's shoulder, and to one side of him. When bringing the horse out of or into a stable, lead him *straight* into the doorway and keep his head low if the lintel is rather low, as this one. This way there will be less danger of knocking his hips on the door jamb or throwing up his head and banging it on the lintel. Such incidents can make horses difficult about these procedures in future.

lead a horse on the footpath even when there are no pedestrians around and even though many feel it is safer in certain circumstances. *Always* walk on the *left* side of the road, on the horse's *off* side. This is essential yet so many people still lead from the near side. By walking on the off side you are between your horse and the traffic and can reassure him. Also, you have more control over him possibly swinging his quarters into the traffic. It must also be said that whereas some motorists might have no compunction about skimming closely past a horse, they will think twice about giving a human such a near miss.

It is wise to carry a long schooling whip in your right hand so that, should you need to keep the quarters in to the left, you can flick them with the whip behind your back without taking your hand off the reins holding up the spare (buckle) end. It is also advisable to wear a fluorescent tabard to make yourself more easily visible to traffic and show that you are traffic-conscious. Ideally, two people should accompany the horse so that help is available should there be trouble. When leading more than one animal, split the convoy into groups of no more than four and preferably less, leading in single file as described, the first and last leaders wearing reflective tabards. There should be at least one person and preferably more *not* leading horses to give control and help direct traffic, if necessary.

At night, lights should be carried as well as reflective clothing worn. Certainly the first and last leaders should have cyclists' arm lights showing white to the front and red to the rear, or a helper should carry a motorist's lantern in the right hand held clearly and slightly out to the side so that motorists are sure to see it. Cyclists' illuminated, battery-operated cross-belts are also a very helpful safety aid whether riding or leading horses in dusk or dark conditions. You really cannot be too careful.

PICKING UP FEET

To pick up a hind foot, first warn the horse that you are going to do something to or with him. Never, whatever you are going to do, go straight to the part needed and get hold of it or start straight off on your work. Always speak to the horse

Picking up a hind foot.

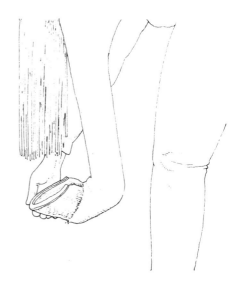

A simple way to help steady a horse is to hold a forefoot up, like this, if someone else needs to do something the horse dislikes, such as pulling (trimming) his tail.

gently and start off at his shoulder with a stroke (horses and ponies find stroking more relaxing and calming than patting, which they may connect with being hit, or kicked by another horse). Run your hand firmly but gently to, in this case, his quarters and, standing with your back to his head, run your nearest hand down the back of his leg. At the hock, run your hand to the front of the joint and down the inside of the leg to the fetlock. Get your fingers under the back of the joint with your palm around the inside of the joint and, leaning slightly against the horse's thigh, to throw his weight off that leg a bit and make it easier for him to lift it, pull the joint up, using the command 'up' at the same time as you pull. Gently but steadily position the foot where you want it but *do not* try to get it too high up or to the side as both these positions can hurt the hip

joint in particular, and any pain or discomfort in any aspect of handling can make the horse more difficult to handle in future. Hold the hoof with your fingers cupped round the wall with your arm in front of his leg: this is so that if he kicks (which will probably be backwards) he won't pull you over. When you've finished, *put* the hoof safely down. Do not just let go, so he can wave it around and maybe tread on you when he stands on it again.

To pick up a fore foot, stroke the horse's neck and, standing at his shoulder with your back to his head, run your nearest hand down the back of the leg, hold the fetlock round the inside, with your fingers round the front of the bone and, leaning against the shoulder, pull the foot upwards at the same time as you say 'up'. Hold the hoof by placing your fingers only under the wall at the toe so he cannot

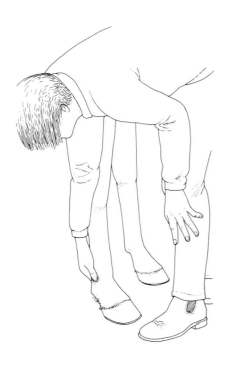

easily lean his weight on you. When you have finished, place the foot on the ground, do not simply let go.

TURNING OUT AND BRINGING IN

To turn a horse out into a field, ideally have a friend with you who can control the gate plus any other animals in the field who may mill round the gateway in curiosity, making your job difficult. If you're alone, place yourself between the horse and the gate so the horse himself

To pick up a front foot, stroke the horse on the shoulder and run your hand down his leg. Grasp the back of the fetlock, lean on his forearm, pull on the fetlock and say 'up' at the same time.

Lead your horse into the field, close the gate behind you and go a few metres into the field.

When you have led your horse into the field, close the gate, turn him back round to face the gate before removing his headcollar. You will then be well out of the way if he should kick with his hind legs.

is next to the gatepost. Hold up the loose end of rope in your leading hand and control the gate with your other hand. Open it wide enough so you can pass through in safety but not so wide that other animals could get out. Do not let go of the gate as it could swing back towards you, or alternatively fall wide open. As the horse goes through the gate, give a gentle pull on the leadrope once his quarters are safely through to bring his head round towards you, saying his name at the same time to keep his attention. Fasten the gate with your 'gate' hand then lead the horse out into the field for a few steps and turn him back round to face the gate. Stand slightly to one side of his head, level with it, and take off the headcollar or unclip the leadrope, after talking to and stroking him for just a few seconds so he doesn't anticipate and get into the

habit of charging off. As you let him go, step backwards towards the gate: he will turn, maybe even whirl round in glee, on his hindquarters and may kick up in excitement at being free and having access to grass, not to mention his friends, but by using this turning-out method you will be safely out of reach of his heels.

To bring a horse in from the field, fasten the gate behind you in case there is any charging about, as otherwise it will provide an escape route. Approach the horse from the side towards his shoulder, calling his name to warn him of your presence and, if necessary, offering a titbit as encouragement. Put on the headcollar or clip on the rope and lead him towards the gate. Position yourself between him and the gate and, as for turning out, use your hand nearest the gate to manipulate it and the other to lead the horse and hold up the spare end of rope. Open the gate just wide enough to get you both through safely and keep hold of the gate. As before, turn his head back towards you once he is through and fasten the gate again. Then, pushing him away from you rather than pulling him round after you (as for leading round a bend), lead him off in the normal way.

STABLE MANNERS

All horses must learn to behave politely and safely in the stable. This is something that they pick up in part as they go along, but which you do need to teach them. They should have learned to stand still on the lunge in response to 'whoa', and must, of course, stand still under saddle when required. If you get the horse to learn that whenever you say 'whoa', whether in stable, field or when ridden, you expect him to stand still, you will save yourself a lot of trouble. To teach him this, start in the box and position him where you want him and the instant he is correct say 'good boy' and stroke his neck. (This should become enough of a reward for him, rather than your having to bribe him constantly with titbits.)

When he moves (as he will eventually), say *immediately* in a stern but not harsh tone of voice 'no' and put him back where he was, then at once stroke him and say 'good boy' again. Eventually he'll get the message that he must stand still, where you say.

To get him to move over in the stable when you are, for example, mucking out, place the flat of your hand on his side where your leg goes when riding and push firmly, saying 'over' at the same time. He may not catch on to start with, but be patient and keep trying saying *only* 'over' as you push. If he is having trouble understanding, get a helper to move the far hind leg out to the side a little, and lean on him as you speak, to help him with weight adjustment and understanding. The instant he moves just one step, praise him.

Going backwards is something he may or may not have learned on the lunge. Most trainers do not teach this, as it allows the horse to realize he can go backwards when working with humans and he may subsequently use it as an evasion before he has learned the habit of obedience. By the time he comes to you, however, he should be well-mannered enough not to evade without justification and you can safely teach him to go back. With a trained horse, you place the flat of your hand on his breast, push and say 'back' at the same time. With a horse who is just learning this, place your hand on his breast, push and say 'back' and at the same time tread gently on his coronets or get a friend to lift a forefoot (or, better, a hind foot as the hind legs usually initiate movement) and move it back at the same time, making it easier for you to push him back and for him to understand. He will probably move back to keep his balance, then you praise him instantly.

MEETING A STRANGE HORSE

Horses have a definite personal space around them which varies but which

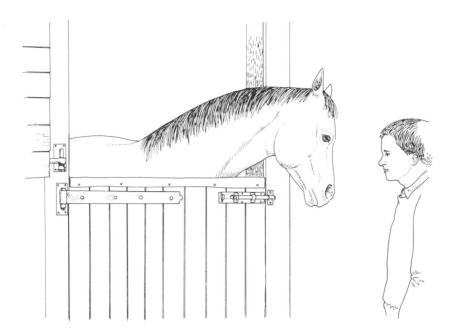

When meeting a strange horse stand a little way from him and talk to him. Let him sniff you before quietly stroking his neck. Never pat a horse on the head – it frightens them. Always ask the horse's attendants whether or not he is safe to approach as some do bite.

Approach a loose horse towards his shoulder rather than from behind, so he can see you easily and will not be startled by your sudden appearance.

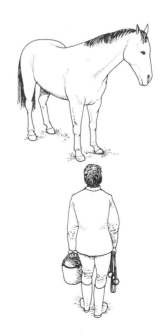

seems to be around 3 m (10 ft) or a bit more with a young or difficult horse. In a stable his personal space is invaded all the time by his handlers, and this is one way of exerting your superiority over him, as he has little choice but to let you approach. With a well-known and well-mannered horse he won't think twice about permitting this, but when approaching a strange horse you cannot take it for granted he will let humans approach, particularly strange ones.

When meeting a horse for the first time it is obviously safer for you if you can do so from outside his box, and let him look out at you approaching over the bottom leaf of the door. Stand slightly to one side about 3 m (10 ft) away and say his name. By all means have a titbit handy if you wish, although it is better to let the horse greet you for yourself rather than for what he can get out of you. He will probably prick his ears and look at you. Confidently but not too quickly, watching for his reaction, approach and stand slightly to the side of his head where he can see you (rather than in front where his vision is

not so clear), about a step from him so he can stretch out his muzzle to smell you. Do not try to touch him at this point. He will possibly sniff your face and shoulders and may start looking in your pockets for titbits. If he seems amenable after several seconds, during which you have spoken quietly to him and used his name if you know it, quietly raise your hand and stroke his shoulder and the bottom of his neck a few times, and finally offer him a titbit. He will now probably remember you if ever you meet again, maybe quite some time into the future and maybe even if he does not show it. There is, however, every excuse for horses used to meeting many people, such as riding-school horses or those at a commercial yard with 'floating' intakes of staff and clients, not to appear to remember most humans.

THE IMPORTANCE OF CONFIDENCE

The main point to remember when dealing with all horses is to cultivate an air of calm confidence. This may not always be easy, particularly if, as you gain experience, you come into contact with difficult horses or even downright nasty ones, but it plays a very large part in being able to cope with them. There is an old saying that horses can smell fear, and this seems

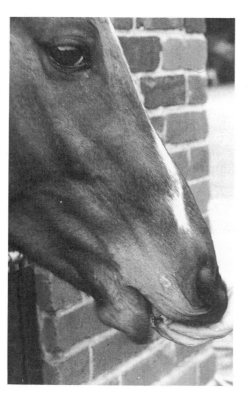

When feeding a horse by hand always keep your fingers and thumb perfectly flat, *not* curved like this. You can see here how easy it is for the horse to catch your fingers with his teeth!

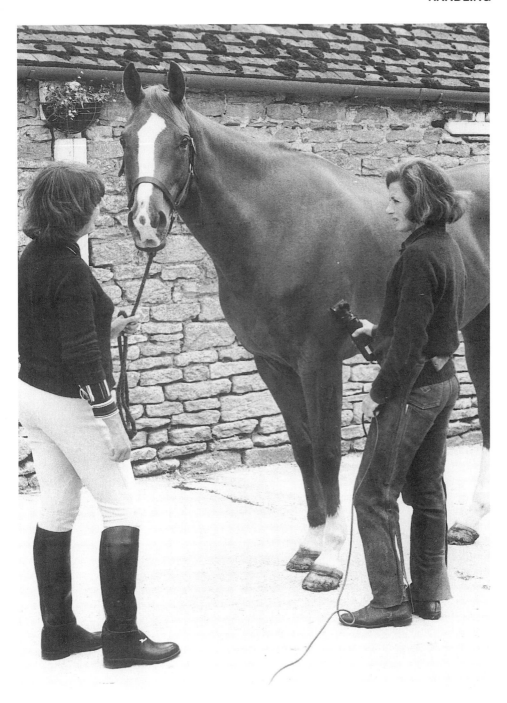

Before starting to clip a horse or pony, even one used to clipping, rest the running clipper on his shoulder like this to warn him of the noise and vibration. Stuffing cotton wool in the ears of a wary or difficult animal often helps calm him down too, as it lessens the noise.

to be true. When we are afraid or even just nervous, we involuntarily give off more perspiration than usual and it contains certain substances which we cannot detect but which animals certainly can. If a horse identifies fear in a human he will react according to his temperament: if he is a dominant horse with little respect for humans he may well react by trying to boss you, subtly or more openly with nips or even bites, squashing you, purposely treading on you, cornering you and so on. If he is a 'follower' type of horse he may become edgy and nervous himself as he thinks there is something around to be frightened of and won't realize it is he himself you are worried about. Well-mannered, sociable horses may show no reaction at all, and schoolmaster-type horses will actually try to put you at your ease.

So if you are nervous tell yourself that you are not; employ mind over matter, breathe deeply and slowly and try to relax and think good thoughts, and you'll have much more chance of handling the horse successfully.

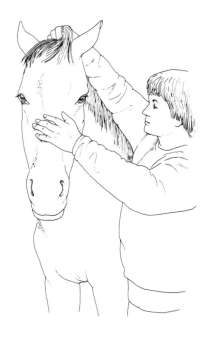

You can lead a quiet horse a short distance in a safe area, if necessary, just by holding his forelock or mane at the poll and steadying his head with a hand on his face. This can also be used as a mild form of restraint.

CHAPTER 7

BADLY HANDLED HORSES

Horses have to be taught to be handled and to respond to bodily and vocally issued requests or commands from humans. It is no secret that the time to start this process is day two of a foal's life. Many people believe in letting the foal get used to the world for a few days before even starting to accustom him to the presence of humans and the feel of even mild contact or restraint, but even after a few days, the foal will have developed a strong sense of being a horse and of humans as alien. Apart from allowing the natural bonding process between mare and foal to take place, usually within about 12 to 24 hours, gentle, non-sentimental handling should begin quickly, not in the form of formal lessons but simply correct handling whenever it is necessary to do anything to mare and foal, such as turning out and bringing in, feeding, checking over, or putting on and taking off foal slips.

Foals should be correctly and gently but firmly handled from their earliest days.

Horse foals in particular soon become big and strong. Handlers are presented with a battle they are not bound to win if the foal has not realized from the start that humans are to be obeyed and are dominant. This is done in a gentle but persistent way, and being a highly specialized subject in the realm of breeding is outside the scope of this book. The important point is never to let the foal realize how physically strong he is, and never to let it win a trial of will and strength. And the only time the

human can be sure of coming out on top is while the foal is still very young. It is often a case of mind over matter, and using physical blocking techniques to condition the foal into thinking that humans are dominant in the 'herd'. Once this is realized resistance occurs less strongly and less often – unless the foal is actually frightened, and then all his primal instincts of self-preservation surface.

The bonding between dam and foal mentioned above is vital to the foal's sense of who and what he is.

When the foal is born, it is best to check him and his dam and then leave them alone as much as possible for 24 hours.

After the first 24 hours normal handling can start and, if it is done properly, by the time the foal is ready to be backed he should be well mannered, socialized to humans and other animals, not least other horses, and able to make his way in the life to which he was born. Unfortunately, many animals do not fall into this category. They are handled too soon, too late, weakly, cruelly, ignorantly or uncaringly, and are full of problems for themselves and all humans who have to do with them.

Good handling, then, is important not only to make the horse amenable and safe for us to live with, but also for the horse's own sake, for without a certain level of manners he will never find a ready home. By teaching a horse manners you are helping not only yourself but also him.

FEAR

Fear is an extremely strong, even over-riding, emotion in most creatures and particularly a prey animal like a horse.

A frightened horse learns nothing helpful and can think of nothing but escaping from the source of his fear or, if cornered, defending himself – and a horse defending himself is a formidable adversary indeed. True, he has no horns or claws, but his teeth and hooves can easily kill a man, and even another horse.

It is easy to provoke fear in the horse, and as far as handling is concerned fear is counter-productive. It is also dangerous. In handling any horse, actual fear should be avoided.

PAIN

Pain is very similar to fear, and can create it. Horses are very sensitive creatures, capable of being severely hurt by a vicious cut from a whip, yet to witness the thrashings some riders, even at the top level of competition, give their horses you would think the horses' hides were made of tanned leather rather than skin, nerves and blood.

There are times when a blow with the whip may be necessary with a downright disobedient, bullying horse to let him know that if he does something he knows is wrong the result will be unpleasant, but repeatedly beating and inflicting pain during 'training' is pointless, cruel and has no part in enlightened horsemanship.

HANDLING TECHNIQUES FOR DIFFICULT HORSES

Even if you, as a novice, are not put into contact with difficult (badly handled) horses, you'll soon become

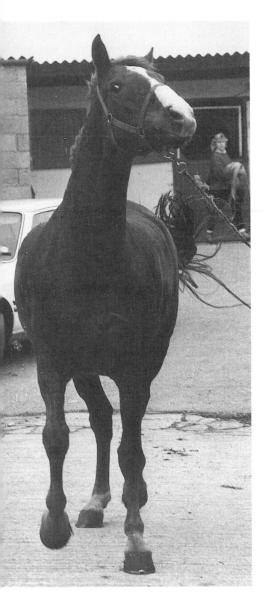

Horses and ponies are easily frightened: it's their nature and part of their very effective survival mechanism. This horse has been startled by something in front of and to his right. He is looking at it with his right eye and throwing up his head, back and to the left, to protect it and – were it not for being held by a lead rope – would be ready to wheel away to his left out of danger.

Use a twitch to quieten fractious horses. The top lip is an accupressure point and the pressure of the twitch releases into the body natural tranquillizers which quieten down the animal until the unpleasant attention, such as cleaning a wound, is over.

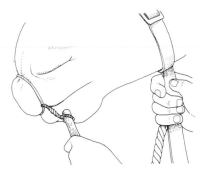

aware that they exist. If you attend a riding centre, for example, you will soon pick up phrases like 'don't go in that bay horse's box – he bites', and so on. As you gain more experience, you will discover that part of learning about horses is having to cope with increasingly difficult ones, and it becomes obvious that by no means all horses are well handled from birth. Many horses have definite 'quirks', even if they are not exactly dangerous. Some horses acquire quirks because of their temperament and not because they have been badly handled. Some, for example, are terrified by flapping polythene covering farm equipment or tacked down the side of buildings, whereas others pay no attention at all to it. The following techniques are offered to help you deal with slightly difficult horses and ponies. 'Hard cases' must be left to the professionals,

Horses who have learned to associate one particular task with discomfort, hassle or pain will, naturally enough, be reluctant to do it in future. Even a small jump like this can cause a refusal if the horse is expecting to be jabbed in the mouth (accidentally or on purpose), stabbed with spurs, whipped or have the rider banging around on his back. Habitual refusers can often be improved by a rest from jumping, followed by correct reschooling and riding. A veterinary check to locate painful injuries (often in the back) is also advised.

for their own and their handlers' sakes.

Head shy horses

This is a fairly common problem and comes about because the horse has either learned that if humans cannot get a bridle or headcollar on him, he will not have to work or submit to handling; or been frightened and hurt by clumsy or downright cruel handling during the process of putting on or taking off a bridle or, less

commonly, a headcollar. The horse waves his nose in the air well out of reach and the novice is completely at a loss as to what to do about it. Most horses, once you have control of their heads, will submit to being bridled and, fortunately, this is quite simple.

With a headcollar, simply place the loose end of the rope over his withers so that it is hanging below his neck on the far side, then get hold of it and hold it with the other end of the rope

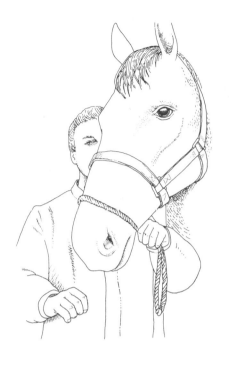

Passing a leadrope round the nose like this gives more control, if held firmly but not painfully, than an ordinary headcollar. However, horses cannot breathe through their mouths, so be careful the rope is not held tight enough to restrict breathing through the nostrils, or the horse might actually panic and become more difficult to handle, not less.

Because horses can easily see behind them and may anticipate pain or discomfort when being handled, they often play up. This can be greatly lessened by preventing them seeing what is going on. For instance, if a horse is being given an injection or having a wound dressed, covering his eye, like this, can often get the job done without too many problems.

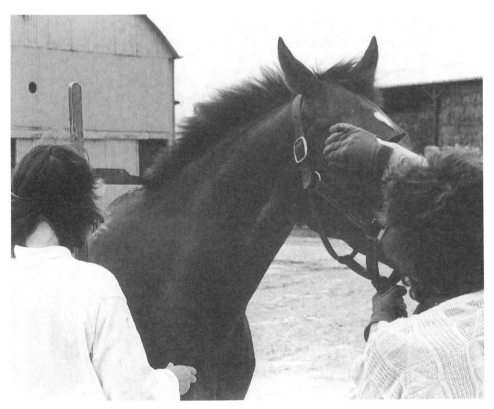

in your right hand. Slide the loop so formed up behind his ears and you have control of his head. You should now be able to put the headcollar on quite easily.

With a bridle, you can unbuckle the reins and pass the right rein up the horse's right shoulder to the withers, re-buckling the reins over the withers so you now have, in effect, put the reins over his head without his realizing it. Again, slide the reins up behind his ears and you have control of his head.

You can also get his nose down by holding the bridle by the cheekpieces and hooking it down with the headpiece.

To put the bridle on a touchy horse, rather than using the normal method of holding the headpiece in your right hand and the bit in your left, put your right arm under his throat and hold both cheekpieces together in your right hand while resting it on the front of his face, so you can control his head. Now bring the bit up to his mouth in the normal way. If he won't open his mouth, use the well-known trick of tickling his tongue inside the corner of his mouth with your left thumb and quickly slip in the bit when he opens up.

When removing the bridle, do let the horse take his time in letting go of the bit. People who snatch out the bit certainly upset, frighten and possibly hurt the horse. Hold the bridle up by the headpiece with the bit supported by the cheekpieces, so that when he lets go the bit does not fall on to his teeth. You can tickle his tongue in the usual way if he seems to take a long time, and gently allow the bit to come

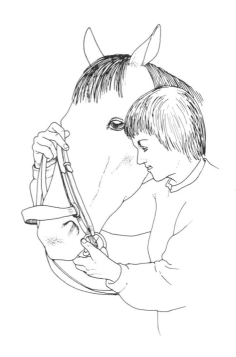

If the horse is slightly difficult to bridle, hold both cheekpieces together with your right hand on the front of his face, like this, so you can control his head, and slip the bit in with your left hand in the usual way. If he won't open his mouth put your thumb into the corner of his mouth (there are no teeth here so you won't be bitten) and tickle his tongue so he'll open up. Then slip in the bit quickly and carefully.

down. Talk to the horse and reassure him all the time. With a straight-bar or mullen-mouthed bit, actually hold it at one end and guide it out of the mouth; this is obviously not so effective with a jointed bit.

Refusing to lead in hand

If you are having trouble persuading a

led horse to go forward, it may be best to seek expert help at once, because the horse may not react to discipline in the way you expect; and, as a led horse is not so easy to control as a ridden one, you could have a lot of problems on your hands.

If the horse seems nervous, get a helper on the other side and if you can spot whatever it is that is upsetting the horse get someone to remove it, if possible. Otherwise, try reassurance with voice and hand, or a lead from another animal.

If the horse is plainly being naughty, a slap under the belly with the flat of your hand may well work. If it doesn't, again, get expert help rather than risk rearing in hand and so on.

To restrain the horse, put a bridle on him, which has more psychological as well as physical control than a headcollar, and have a schooling whip in your outside hand. Stand the horse alongside something firm such as a safe fence or brick wall. Stand at his shoulder and hold the reins (over his head) in the usual way. At the same time as you give the command 'walk on' flick his flank or thigh with the long whip behind your back. A very few horses will respond by actually pulling back or half-rearing; most of them will move forward sharply, so be ready and don't undo your good work by getting left behind and jabbing him in the mouth. Go with him, walk on for a few paces, halt and repeat. A very few lessons of this will result in a willing leader, and if he does offer to refuse again just put your hand behind your back (whip or no whip) and he'll probably skip forward expecting a flick. Do say 'good boy' when he co-operates.

Refusing to be saddled

Horses who don't like being saddled may have been hurt during the process, usually by being girthed up too tightly and too quickly, or by having their skin pinched. In some cases, they may have been hurt by an ill-fitting saddle and come to associate wearing a saddle with pain. Horses which 'sink' down or back away when the saddle is put on their back are said to suffer from 'cold back'. This is an old-fashioned expression stemming from a belief that the horse simply objected to the cold feel of leather on his back. In fact, horses who appear to resent the saddle are much more likely to be suffering from back pain, probably caused by muscular or spinal injury, and need veterinary help and possibly physiotherapy rather than having the saddle warmed before it is put on.

If you come across a horse who dislikes being saddled, it is probably best not to persevere but to tell someone expert such as a riding instructor.

If the horse will let you saddle him but resents having the girth done up, do it up very gradually one hole at a time. When the girth is tight enough to keep the saddle on as you mount (so that you can fit the edges of your flat fingers between it and the horse), pull the horse's legs forward from the knee to stretch out the skin wrinkles which may have formed so that they do not hurt the horse. The horse who is difficult to girth up may 'blow himself out' against the girth, and once mounted you may have to girth up more holes than with other horses.

The important point to remember is never to haul up the girth obviously

Most horses love loose schooling, over jumps or on the flat. Lack of exercise is often a cause of a horse being 'difficult'. This is one way of not only teaching a horse to jump or otherwise exercise, without the hindrance of a rider, and also to obey a voice, but also of allowing a horse to let off steam, particularly when outdoor exercise is restricted due to bad ground conditions. All-weather, outdoor loose schooling areas are also a very useful facility to create.

very tightly as this causes discomfort and resentment in the horse. If you are uncertain as to how tight a girth should be, seek expert help.

Horses who will not stand for attention or walk co-operatively

Sometimes a headcollar and rope may not be enough to steady a horse being held for attention or led about. A quick way to obtain more control is simply to wrap the leadrope over his nose and hold it in a loop round the nose, your hand under his jaw. You can also pass the rope through the two side 'D's of the headcollar and tighten the pressure of the noseband that way, holding the rope together, again, with your hand beneath the jaw.

A horse who will not stand still can be gently restrained by someone holding up a leg, usually a foreleg, while you work, just as if he or she were going to pick out the foot. Another simple method is to put an elastic band round the base of one ear so that it fits snugly and the horse can feel it but not so tight that it is uncomfortable. This seems to work by giving the horse something extra to think about, so distracting him from what you are doing.

Horses who rush off when led in hand and pull you along with them, or who charge out of (or into) the stable, may be restrained by jerks on the headcollar noseband via the leadrope; one long pull will not be effective. Otherwise, slap them fairly hard on the breast with the flat of your hand saying 'whoa', or whatever they understand for slowing down. The instant they do it again, repeat the treatment. One good crack with a riding whip or stick is also effective (on the breast), but not a good hiding or mauling their heads. If you still have trouble, consult an expert.

WHY RESCHOOLING CAN TAKE A LONG TIME

Horses are creatures of habit and once something is learned it can be very difficult to get them to change their behaviour pattern. This works for good and bad behaviour, and is a good reason for getting it right from the start. Old habits die hard, but with persistence and consistent handling and treatment, so that the horse always knows what to expect, you can effect a considerable improvement in most horses.

It is important to realize that many difficult horses are that way because they have no confidence in their handlers, or have never been taught to behave properly. They are acting out of self-defence or simply because they do not know any better. There are horses, however, who are just trying to boss their handlers. Having a dominant temperament and having got away with it in the past, they know being 'difficult' works, so they naturally keep trying it on.

In both cases, persistence and consistent, determined handling can really improve matters, but if matters are handled wrongly the horse can become resentful, bitter, maybe even dangerous, and even more convinced that humans are *persona non grata*. If in doubt at all about your ability to handle or retrain a particular horse, always seek and be prepared to pay for expert help.

CHAPTER 8

INTELLIGENCE AND LEARNING

General intelligence in horses and ponies has already been established, and horses learn very quickly if the trainer understands their mentality and how to put things over to them.

In the wild horses had to learn quickly about their environment and how several aspects of it affected their comfort and survival – where the water-holes were, who was in charge of the herd, what non-horse animals were a threat, where to shelter from extremes of weather and from flies. The very first thing a foal learns is who his mother is, what she smells like, sounds like, looks like and tastes like. This vital lesson can be learned within a very few hours, remarkable when it is considered that the foal has absolutely no experience at all of the outside world. As in humans, some experts believe that foals learn the sound of their mother's voice from inside the womb, although this can probably never be tested.

It is said that a foal has learned over 75 per cent of what it needs to know by the time it is a year old – how to manipulate its limbs at all paces and in all positions, how to suckle, graze and drink water, how to scratch itself either with a hoof or rubbing on a tree, as well as, in domestication, what humans are, what artificial food is

(although, of course, it will not perceive it as artificial), where to find water in the paddock or stable, what the yard routine is, and so on. This is all vital to its ability to cope with and adapt to life.

Horses are said to learn by association of ideas. They connect a particular situation or sound with a particular result or action. When the same situation or sound occurs in future, they will, sooner rather than later, expect the same result or action as occurred before. This places a great burden on the trainer to make sure his horse comes across as few unpleasant experiences as possible, and to be certain that when schooling and handling the horse he is utterly consistent both as to the treatment of the horse and in the way he gives commands and aids, right down to body position. Horses are acutely observant, and have excellent memories (another legacy from their wild ancestry), and they will eventually respond to the tiniest shift in body movement or weight adjustment, or the position on the ground of the trainer.

Imagine a horse hacking along a road, quite calm and well behaved, when suddenly a piece of paper is blown up off the pavement into his

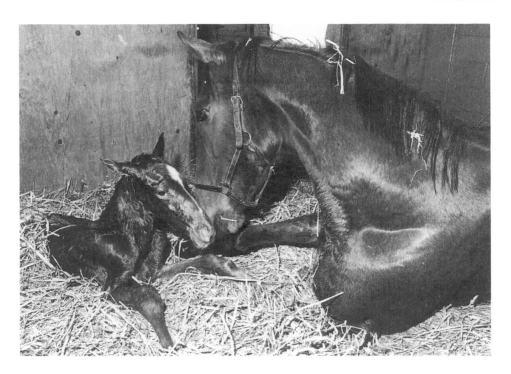

Like human babies, foals start learning while in the womb, and start learning about their new environment the instant they are born. The first and most important thing to learn is, who Mum is; the second is how to stand up, and the third is where to find the milk bar.

face, frightening and temporarily blinding him. He will probably stop and whirl round or toss his head, maybe rearing or doing whatever his now panic-stricken brain commands. Once the paper is disposed of he eventually calms down, although maybe not to the extent of his previous state. The horse will remember the incident as regards both to what happened and where. He will possibly become suspicious of all things that look like pieces of paper on the floor, and will almost certainly get edgy and probably shy whenever he passes that particular spot again on the same rein. The location and incident are 'locked' into his mind.

However, when approaching the spot from the opposite direction he may not react at all because the place looks different. (Remember he looks at things with one eye on most occasions.) He has learned, quite dramatically for him, that pieces of paper and things that look like them, are likely to jump up and blind him. This is a wild instinct and it will take a long time and much calming and reassurance from his rider to get over it to the extent where he does not react to a similar set of circumstances in that way again. However, he will never forget it completely and will, probably for the rest of his life, associate that place and pieces of paper with fear.

The incident could have been much worse, of course. He could have been involved in an accident with a vehicle on the road. Again, he will have learned that motor vehicles mean great pain, and if he was traffic-proof before he probably never will be again, for it takes only one painful or unpleasant experience with a car, tractor, bus, earth-mover or whatever to ruin a horse's behaviour in traffic permanently, even under the most expert management.

Because horses learn so completely and quickly, it is essential to try to get things right with them every time. Everyone makes mistakes, but generally the rider or handler who habitually has a calm, consistent attitude and who can retain presence of mind has a much better chance of teaching their horse that if he takes his cue from the human he will be all right, especially when he panics in a difficult situation. However, there will

Initial work on the lunge forms a standard part of most horses' basic training. Horses are very susceptible to the sound of the human voice, both the sounds it makes and its inflection and tone. It is essential that you give commands in exactly the same way every time – this includes vocal praise such as 'good boy' or reprimands such as a sternly-said 'no' – if the horse is to learn to associate a particular word or phrase with a particular movement or gait. To him the words themselves mean nothing: he depends entirely on the nature of the sound, so consistency is vital.

be times when he will not be all right. If a dog runs up and bites the horse this is quite outside your control.

Horses take their cues from humans, whether good or bad, and most of them are clever enough to realize that pleasing humans is a sensible thing to do. This is why badly-trained horses are more difficult and time-consuming to school than completely green ones. Usually they can be improved, although they soon revert to their previous behaviour when the appropriate circumstances arise.

When educating any horse, it's a good plan to use the services of a schoolmaster (reliable, trained) horse to guide him. Horses do also take their cues from each other probably more than even a trusted human. Worldly-wise horses will not follow the lead of a giddy youngster, but they can teach and calm them.

If young horses can be allowed to watch older, trained ones being lunged, ridden and handled, they certainly learn faster than those who have never seen this sort of activity before, and it is common practice for a trained horse to give a reluctant one a lead over a ditch or jump, say, out hacking or hunting. The horse will often follow a colleague where he will not follow a human, or be led by one.

Horses, of course, do not have the same kind of sound language that humans do: they do not understand English either, but respond to the actual sound and the way it is spoken, the inflection and tone of the voice being what they listen for. Because of this, it is essential that trainers use exactly the same words and tones every time when schooling horses,

A good type of lungeing cavesson. The metal strip down the front of the face helps stabilise it and the cheekpieces are so arranged that they do not pull round and rub against the horse's eye, a common fault.

young or old, so that they come to associate that sound with a particular movement.

When starting off a youngster on the lunge, for example, start by leading him around the circle, giving the command 'walk on' (which he should already know from being handled from a foal); then say 'whoa' (which he should also know) as you stop. Gradually continue, walking and halting, taking yourself further and further away from him, until you are in the centre of the circle and he is walking and stopping on the circle at the end of the lunge line, purely in response to your voice. He can be taught his other movements in the same way, although some trainers use a helper to lead the horse round the

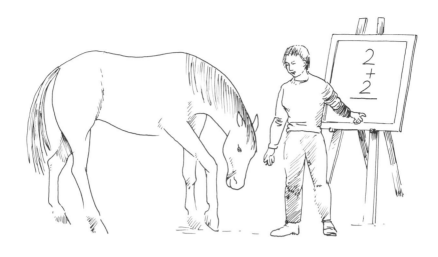

'The Intelligent Horse', Clever Hans, would tap out numbers and do other amazing tricks simply by closely watching and reacting to his trainer's most minute movements, often given unconsciously by the trainer, who genuinely believed he had taught Hans to count. Hans simply stopped tapping when he saw his trainer relax as the correct number was reached.

circle for guidance, leaving the trainer to give the actual commands. Others believe this confuses the horse, but it is a matter of personal opinion and experience. The aim, either way, is to get the horse used to the command for each gait or action.

Once the horse has learned the various commands, be consistent with your use of them. If you try giving commands in a different way, with a different inflection or tone, you may well find that not only does the horse not respond, but also that he becomes confused and worried because he does not know what you want. This is not stupidity. To him, you are now speaking a totally different language from the one that you have taught him: he cannot possibly be expected to understand and do what you want.

PUNISHMENT AND REWARD

A lot is heard about punishment and reward teaching. The old school believed in punishing the horse, however mildly, whenever he responded incorrectly to an aid or command. For example, if a trainer was trying to teach the horse to strike off in right canter and the horse persistently did so in left canter, the horse would be punished by whip or spur, or both. Some trainers even believed that the horse would only learn what to do by being punished for doing what was not wanted.

The more prevalent school of thought today is to praise the horse when he gets a response right and do nothing when he gets it wrong, or simply say 'no' or something similar (another command he should have become used to from foalhood) to let him know that this is not what you want. To hit or even verbally berate a horse who is trying to guess what you want is stupid and cruel.

Anyone who wants to be a successful trainer or handler of horses should realize the importance of putting a horse in a position where it is easy, not just possible, for him to get his response right – give aids when the horse's legs are positioned correctly for him to strike off in the new gait, or whatever – otherwise, if the horse physically cannot respond, you'll never get the right response and the horse will become upset, or angry.

To either correct or reward a horse, probably the point which is as important as being consistent is that of administering your praise or correction the instant the horse responds. The horse's brain operates such that he must receive the sound and the action, or reaction, within a second, or at the very most, two seconds, for him to connect the two. After this time lapse he will not relate the two and your praise or punishment will mean nothing.

The following is an example of bad

Horses quicky learn that certain things can be painful, such as a rider being 'left behind' at a jump, like this, and jabbing a horse in the mouth. They may begin to associate jumping with pain and start to refuse jumps, or refuse to do whatever it is that causes them pain.

disciplining. A rider was standing talking to a friend when her horse, for no apparent reason, suddenly gave her arm quite a hard nip. The woman reacted, as expected, by giving a yelp and then examining and nursing her arm. The horse, by this time, was gazing off into the distance oblivious of her owner, who then, after fully five or six seconds, began slapping the horse across the face several times. She then examined her arm again, and slapped the horse yet again! The horse was obviously alarmed and upset at being slapped across the face. This horse did *not* learn from this experience that nipping is wrong: what she did learn was that her owner was prone to unkind, irrational behaviour and this is damaging to the bond of confidence and mutual trust which must exist between horse and human if a satisfactory relationship is to be created.

Similarly, when a horse does something right, always say at once 'good boy' in a very pleased tone the instant he does well. This goes not only for correctly executed actions on the lunge but under saddle, too. It's all the same to the horse. He needs to know when he's getting it right whether you're sitting on him or not.

It is also rather late to pat and praise a horse several seconds after, for example, he has completed a show-jumping round. On the other hand, a quiet 'good boy' as he takes a jump, as some riders are heard to do, is very appropriate. If you want to get through to the horse that he is doing well, tell him at once, not several seconds afterwards when it will not sink in. Fuss and affection are fine any time: reward must be instant.

On the same topic, how infuriating it is to see riders giving their horses a crack with the whip *after* they have taken off at a jump. This action indicates in no uncertain terms to the horse that he is doing wrong! So, incidentally, does being jabbed in the mouth during a jump or, intentionally or otherwise, stabbed by the spurs. Any painful or unpleasant action will

It is important to praise the horse when he does something good, such as walking through a puddle, which some horses dislike. The praise should be instant, otherwise the horse will not connect the praise with the act and will never learn what pleases you.

It's often a big help to have an assistant when teaching a horse a new movement. Here a young horse is being taught to back and the assistant is reinforcing the vocal command by pushing him on the breast. If the horse has already been taught this without a rider, say in the box as part of his stable manners, the task will be that much easier.

be associated by the horse with the act of jumping and it is a miracle more of them do not start refusing or becoming nappy when jumping when one really studies the techniques of some riders.

Horses, then, are very quick, able learners, but they learn 'right' and 'wrong' just as effectively. The watchwords are *consistency*, *timing* and *repetition*, along with copious doses of simplicity and patience. Keep your commands simple, preferably no more than three syllables, and do not lose your commands among a stream of other words as this makes it virtually impossible for the horse to pick out the meaningful sounds from a stream of noise.

Be prepared to repeat your words and actions, parrot-fashion, until the horse does what you want. The more consistent you are the quicker he will learn. Soon he will try to second-guess you and do what you want almost as soon as you ask him, if not before.

CHAPTER 9

DISCIPLINE

An undisciplined horse in a domestic environment is totally unacceptable. It is useless from a work point of view, dangerous to the humans who have to handle it (if they can get near it), and dangerous to people and other animals in its vicinity.

Discipline is not a purely human concept alien to horses. In fact, it comes naturally to horses to be disciplined, as they are subject to it from the first day of their lives. For a foal's first few weeks with its dam, she will keep it away from other horses for the most part, except possibly her near relatives and close friends in the herd. And during this time, she will teach it discipline.

However, there is discipline of another kind, which is natural and essential for a well-balanced individual to be able to relate to and live with his herd mates – the discipline imposed by the herd hierarchy. Every herd has its leader, its high-ups and those lower down. Newcomers (fairly rare in nature except for those born into the herd) have to learn their place, often after much painful and distressing initiation, and although new foals in a herd excite interest among the other horses, a foal quickly learns that it by no means gets its own way.

Horse herds do not operate an 'aunty' system as, for example, elephants. Each dam and foal unit is very much the centre of its own universe within the herd. If the foal tries to suckle from another lactating mare it will almost certainly be sent packing in no uncertain terms. Provided the foal treats other mares as herd members without actually trying to muscle in on their attention and affection all will be fine, but if it gets pushy it will be put in its place. Other mares certainly won't help a pushy foal if it is in trouble.

Even among themselves, foals have a hierarchy and this depends as much on personality as on physical size and condition. Any animal which is sickly or injured can expect to be picked on by the others as they see this as an ideal opportunity to move up the hierarchy. Foals weigh each other up and slot each other into place, and, as they get older, spend less and less time with their dams and more time socializing with each other.

But there are, in a natural herd, other age groups as well as foals and adults. The previous year's foals will be yearlings, and these will be of both sexes. Sometime between the yearling and two-year-old stage the young males will either leave the herd or be booted out by the resident stallion (who stays with his mares all year round). This leaves two-year-old and three-year-old females as well as male foals and yearlings, plus mature mares (four years upwards) and the stallion.

The foals start investigating other herd members, and it is woe betide any foal who tries to get the better of an animal of an older generation. It is swiftly put in its place none too gently. Mature mares, particularly once they have ceased suckling their foals significantly, are quite tolerant of other mares' foals. It seems to be the younger generation, the yearlings, two and three-year-olds, who mete out the natural discipline so essential to a well-balanced outlook, although mature mares will certainly do so if a particular foal is getting troublesome.

As they grow up, then, foals are perfectly used to being castigated and reprimanded by their elders, and develop a healthy, natural respect for them. Few herds in domesticated conditions are allowed to develop this kind of discipline, apart from in feral herds kept in fairly natural surroundings, such as are found in eastern Europe (Hungary and Poland operate this system successfully, as do some of the horse-owning peoples on the steppes of eastern Asia), and also

A newly-foaled mare and her foal should be left alone as much as is practically possible, to allow natural bonding to take place – usually about 12 to 24 hours. The foal can be gently helped to its feet and guided towards the udder if the foal seems to be taking an unreasonably long time to do these things for itself. Correct, sympathetic handling should start from day two of the foal's life, so that human superiority and discipline become second nature to it. This can also prevent assertive mares trying to dominate humans handling her and her foal.

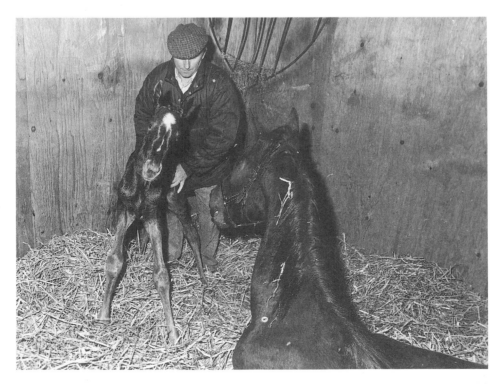

Mares often discipline their own foals quite sharply to let them know what sort of behaviour is acceptable and what is not. Novice breeders often make the mistake of letting foals get away with undesirable behaviour, the foals grow up not knowing what is acceptable behaviour and become difficult and dangerous to handle.

to some extent in America (particularly the west) and Australia. Even here, however, it is often the case that animals of different age groups are separated into different herds.

Where truly all-age herds are maintained it is very noticeable how well-mannered the youngsters are before they have any significant training from humans. They come to hand very much quicker than more artificially-reared youngsters, seem to learn quicker, do not need correcting so much and do not seem to go through that rebellious phase experienced by many young horses. They also seem quieter, calmer, more

worldly-wise and certainly more accepting of discipline, when needed. By the time they come to being backed and ridden or driven they are more fully aware that good behaviour is a way of life.

This type of natural discipline does not occur in domesticity where the normal intensive stud policy is practised of splitting foals after weaning into groups or herds, or even only pairs, of single ages and single sexes. For instance, two or more weanling fillies will be kept together, two or more yearling colts and so on. This pairs system is even worse than a group of same-age/sex animals because no matter how carefully they are paired up one will always come out on top, such being the nature of things. This means that the top one will probably get a superiority complex while the underdog never develops its self-confidence as fully as it might, as it never has the experience of being superior to anything. And if anything is needed in today's competitive horse world it is self-confidence.

In professional studs and yards run by knowledgeable, sensitive horsemen and women, the problems caused through this separation system may be adequately overcome by means of systematic, well-judged handling and training. However, the apparently fairly high number of difficult young horses around is due partly to restrictive rearing, combined with sub-standard early handling practices. In more natural domestic herds where humans regularly handle, check over and bring the horses in and out, the youngsters automatically come to accept humans as part of their lives and routines, and realize that, like

Many domesticated horses are difficult to handle because they have never been correctly disciplined when young, either by being allowed to live in a natural herd situation and be disciplined by older herd members, or because their human handlers have let them get away with bad (if natural) behaviour such as kicking or biting. Young horses receive unmistakable harsh discipline from their elders in natural herds and this actually makes them easier for humans to handle, too.

dominant horses, they are to be respected. Obviously, once the males reach puberty they have to be separated from the rest of the herd if unwanted pregnancies are to be avoided, but this, too, is perfectly natural. If reared together from birth there is no need to force young colts to lead subsequent solitary lives, as usually happens in domestic breeding establishments. In the wild, they roam, meet up with other ousted colts and young and old stallions and, as there is no harem to fight for, they live together in bachelor bands quite amicably after the usual jockeying for position in the hierarchy. Stallions do not habitually fight until death or serious injury results: this would be uneconomic in nature, where the need to survive is everything. The underdog admits defeat and leaves the mares to his superior. Where there are no mares there is no real fighting.

Young colts kept in domestic herds are happier, less stressed and calmer than when they are kept singly in paddocks deprived of natural social

Horses, whether working or resting, are better off when kept in groups provided there is no out-and-out bully who may injure others or harrass them unreasonably. Horses will always find their own levels in their natural hierarchy, and be much calmer, more content and easily handled and ridden. They have the advantage of close company and social interaction, plus more space and freedom to move about. Covered yards like this can be made to open into a paddock so the horses can be allowed grazing, or not, as required.

interaction. They also grow up more mannerly, having experienced both herd and peer discipline and also human handling from birth, and are ultimately more respectful of their mares when used at stud.

HUMAN DISCIPLINE

Having discussed at some length discipline between horses, what about the sort with which we are more familiar, that which humans mete out to horses? Probably the two most important points are that discipline must be absolutely instant, and fair. If it is not instant, as already explained, the horse will not understand that he has offended our human standards and will not come to associate the deed with pain and be put off doing it again. To punish a horse over severely, as is often seen in humans who like to show that they are 'boss' over a big, strong animal, is unfair.

It is essential that any punishment is given consistently. For example, if a horse has a habit of kicking, but is only punished for it sometimes, he will never learn whether it is acceptable or not to kick. In a horse herd, he will soon find out which horses he can get away with kicking and which he cannot, because some will kick back. In human society, he has to learn that he may not kick *any* human, or other animal (including other horses when under saddle or led, that is, when he is under human control). It is impossible to stop him kicking other horses when turned out with them as natural manners then take over. However, if he is an invariable troublemaker, kicking and biting his field-mates habitually, the natural *status quo*

should be interfered with and the culprit turned out alone or just with an animal or animals who are dominant to him and whom he does not kick. If he is left with horses that he kicks, they will be miserable and could be seriously hurt. Broken bones frequently arise from kicks.

When horses are handled and ridden by more than one person, all concerned must be aware of 'punishment rules' – instantly and every time, otherwise the horse will become resentful and confused, which destroys essential confidence and trust.

WHAT CONSTITUTES PUNISHMENT?

Short, sharp shocks are the order of the day when horses need punishment. It is debatable whether or not they ever come to understand actual right and wrong. Many experts feel that horses simply associate a particular action with a particular result. If they kick they are hit, either with a whip or a slap both of which are unpleasant and/or painful. They thus learn that kicking means pain and they usually stop. They don't actually grasp that it is wrong because in their natural life there is no right and wrong so they can have no concept of it.

Other experts maintain that horses, and other animals, come to learn very well what pleases us and what displeases us, but this is still not exactly right and wrong. Whatever the true situation, the fact is, fortunately, that horses can be trained to do what pleases us and to refrain from doing what displeases us. It is interesting to watch a horse's reaction when he is, say, playing up a student

Two horses having a kicking match. This can be dangerous if the horses are shod. Although this behaviour is natural when horses are defending themselves or sorting out their positions in the herd hierarchy, known kickers should not be turned out with other animals for fear of serious injury to their victims.

in his box who is trying to do something to him and despite all her cajoling and reprimanding she is getting nowhere. Along comes a senior member of staff, or even a more advanced student, who gives the horse a few sharp words and he submits to the original student with a chastened look on his face. Has he accepted he was doing 'wrong', or does he simply associate the second

person with dominance?

Whatever the answer, there is no doubt that in practice instant, quick 'punishment' (for want of a better word) is the most effective. One sharp crack of the whip the moment a horse does wrong gets the message through to him in no uncertain terms; one hard slap on the belly or even just one crossly-spoken (not shouted) word, probably 'no' or a harsh growl: these are all quite clear to the horse, especially if the voice and physical punishment are used at the same time. After this, it will soon be possible just to use the voice to punish the horse, although a dominant, wilful horse

When disciplining a horse you must do it immediately after the offence or at the same time, if you can, so he associates the punishment with the act and will learn what is not wanted and results in unpleasantness. Here a horse is biting someone and receiving an unpleasant slap on the belly, instantly, for his pains.

may sometimes still need a physical reminder.

What should never be administered is a sustained beating, because by the time it is over the horse will surely have forgotten what all the pain is for and punishment then degenerates into cruelty. Another unforgiveable technique is to jab the horse in the mouth as this is overly-painful and will make the horse hard-mouthed, head-shy and bitter. Spurs, too, should be used with great discretion, the blunt variety being just as capable of inflicting unreasonable pain as the sharp ones. They should not be used as a punishment at all, but as an augmenting aid.

Different horses react to punishment in different ways. Some horses simply will not tolerate being touched with a whip, probably because they remember past whippings and remember how painful they were. Remember that the horse can see the whip being carried and used out of his side-set eye, and some horses will not even co-operate with a rider who is simply carrying one. They may, however, succumb to discipline as a result of a sharply administered word, and for many this is enough.

If everyone considering using a whip on a horse, especially the cutting whip variety, hit themselves just once on the leg, even through their breeches, as hard as they intend to hit the horse, they might well change their mind, at least about the severity of the intended blow. The horse's skin is just as sensitive as ours (he can feel a fly land even through his hair coat); in fact many scientists believe that horses have a lower pain threshold than humans.

SELF-ADMINISTERED 'DISCIPLINE'

Another extremely effective form of discipline is that which is self-administered. An example might be the horse who runs backwards when you try to mount him. If you position him so that he runs into something very unpleasant but harmless, such as a holly bush, you will find that this habit stops most expeditiously. Never, however, run the horse into anything that is potentially injurious such as a pile of rubble, a barbed-wire fence or down into a ditch (which can severely injure his back).

A useful cure for biting is to sew two wire dog-grooming mitts on to the

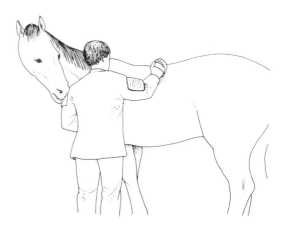

Self-inflicted 'punishment' seems to be effective in teaching horses what not to do. Here wire dog grooming mits sewn on the to the groom's jacket will give the horse a nasty prick on a sensitive area of his muzzle as he tries to bite the groom's arm. The horse will learn that biting causes him pain and will be less inclined to do so in future.

upper arms of an old jacket and wear it when grooming or handling the horse. As he turns his head to bite, push your upper arm towards his muzzle so that he gets a nasty prick on a very sensitive part, and, again, he will probably stop this habit quite quickly. He won't associate the discomfort with you if you ignore him and carry on doing whatever you were doing and will, therefore, not resent you. Of course, gentle grooming will help.

This type of discipline is akin to the way in which a horse learns about his natural environment, and seems to sink in.

Discipline and punishment can easily go wrong if administered by people who do not really understand what they are doing. Sadly, this applies to many very experienced horsepeople so it is difficult for the novice to know where to turn for help. If you remember that timing (instant administration, waiting no more than one second) and fairness (consistency, administered every time so the horse knows where he stands) are vital elements in disciplining horses, this will help you greatly. Most importantly, never let anyone beat your horse or punish him more than one second after a misdemeanour. Finally, never punish a hard-to-catch horse once you have finally caught him, to 'teach him a lesson', as he'll think coming to you is 'wrong'. It's logical when you think about it; reward him instead.

CHAPTER 10

THE HORSE'S FEELINGS

People often say that ponies and horses do not have expressive faces; that they are less expressive than dogs, for example. However, this is not necessarily so. They do use body language to communicate more than humans do, whereas humans use their voices most. With experience, close contact and sensitivity it is quite possible to judge a horse's feelings by his face, body and general aura.

Horses cannot be treated like motor-bikes, to be shut away and forgotten, with no attention to their physical or mental needs, until they are wanted again. They need regular

Horses usually feel more content when given space and visibility, as they feel safer when they can see more and have room to move. Individual stables are a completely unnatural method of housing horses, causing many to become frustrated, stressed and neurotic. Low-level stress is often not noticed by the horse's handlers, who may assume the horse is perfectly all right.

Not many families want their horse on the hearthrug with them, although miniatures such as Falabellas are known to share their owners' houses. Because horses are denied as close an association with their owners as are dogs for example they cannot be expected to form as strong a bond, although there are exceptions.

contact with other horses, and come to appreciate contact with humans they trust and respect. Humans are as much a part of their lives as other horses, and while we expect them to learn our language and, in certain cases, make allowances for our emotions and feelings, we often take precious little trouble to learn how they communicate, or consider whether or not they are in the mood for work or are feeling a bit off mentally or physically. Yet there is no doubt that horses communicate their feelings both to humans and to other animals; we just do not always recognize what they are saying, or sometimes that they are saying anything at all.

People have argued for generations about whether or not horses actually feel love for humans in the way dogs do. Dogs are certainly closer to us in their social lifestyle. Both are gregarious predators with similar social and family structures. They co-operate and help and protect each other, and it may be these likenesses that link humans more closely to dogs than to horses. Some say that humans cannot be as close to horses as to dogs as they do not actually live with them, but many dogs are consigned to an outdoor kennel. The Bedouin Arabs, however, did and occasionally still do live with their horses, who may actually inhabit the same tent as the family. Ask anyone who has undertaken a long, arduous trek, particularly through isolated regions, and they will say that a much closer affection, if not actually love, does seem to come from their horse than when contact is more limited. It may be argued that this is simply self-preservation on the part of the horse: he regards the human as his link with safety, food, water, maybe the only other acceptable living thing for miles around, or the only one who regularly makes him feel good, feeds him, and seems to cater to his comforts. A horse, I feel, thinks and behaves towards humans and himself more

like a cat. He is much more independent of mind than a dog.

However, because of this independence of mind, it is all the more flattering and pleasing when a horse obviously shows he is pleased to see you. Horses are excellent teachers if you pay attention to what they are saying via their behaviour and treatment of you. If I see a horse expressing dislike of a particular person I am always suspicious of them!

Mares obviously have a strong bond with their foals and it is known that female horses form strong lifelong ties between mothers and daughters, and to a lesser extent with sisters and aunts. Perhaps they would with their

Horses often form close friendships with animals of other species, and individually-stabled horses may particularly appreciate visits and company from other residents of their yard.

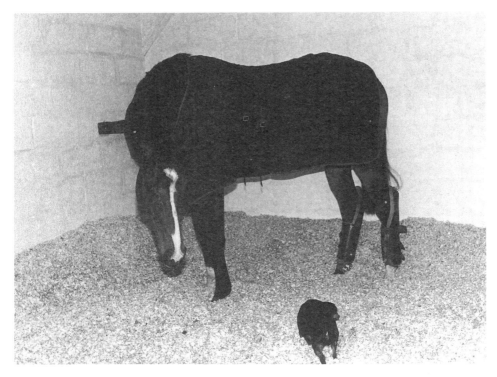

sons if they were allowed to stay in the natural herd but, feral or domesticated, they are separated when quite young. There is no doubt that many mares and foals have a terrible time during the weaning process usually inflicted on them in domesticity. Perhaps they get over it quicker than a human mother and child would, but perhaps it is unduly arrogant of humans to suggest that this is not really love.

As for love between a mare and a stallion, if it exists it is certainly short-lived. There is the normal desire to breed, but once the mare conceives she is not only supremely indifferent to the stallion, she shows active dislike. In-foal mares in natural herds often show complete indifference to the stallion, whereas others will occasionally socialise non-sexually with him. As for his feelings, he is naturally promiscuous and does not show love for any particular mare, although naturally-living stallions are known to show concern and affection for their mares in some cases.

As for other emotions, horses certainly experience fear and alarm and exhibit them readily because of their nature. They also show anger, anxiety, anticipation, happiness (although some dispute this),

In natural conditions the herd stallion is not the herd leader but will stay with his 'wives' and offspring all year round, socializing with them and preventing them being stolen by other stallions. Stallions and their families can become very affectionate and companionable even outside the breeding season.

enjoyment, excitement, submission or defeat and, who knows, any of the other emotions that humans and other animals experience. No one can penetrate horses' minds to find out for certain how they are feeling or how they view their lives with us, but they do give a lot away by means of physical expression – body language.

BODY LANGUAGE OF THE HORSE

This is a fascinating subject about which entire books have been written. Many of us absorb our horses' body language without thinking about it, especially if we have been brought up with horses from an early age. Those who come to horses later in life may have more trouble recognizing what their horses are feeling or are trying to say.

The most obvious place to look to find out what a horse is feeling is his head. It also provides an excellent guide to his temperament and, therefore, is important when assessing a horse for purchase – few people want a nasty-tempered horse unless it is exceptionally talented and they are professional enough to cope with it.

The horse should take a healthy interest in life, with his ears flicking to and fro towards whatever is capturing his attention. The ears are excellent indicators of this and can work independently; a ridden horse, for example, often flicks one ear back to listen to his rider while the other is pricked forward on the route ahead.

The eyes are also very good indicators to temperament. They should have a kind, calm look, but may also show excitement, tension or

fear and other emotions. It is not easy for a novice to guess accurately the look in a horse's eyes, but close study and experience, along with expert on-the-spot guidance, if available, will soon yield results.

The horse's nostrils will flare round and open when excited and he may snort down them. They will obviously also flare when he is out of breath after work, or in distressed breathing due to disease, and are important to the horse as he cannot breathe through his mouth. In anger, the nostrils may be wrinkled slightly up and back, as they will be when he is in pain. Normally, when the horse is calmly resting or eating, they will be relaxed and half open.

The tail varies with the horse's breeding and is more loftily carried in 'hot' breeds such as the Thoroughbred and Arabian. Usually, a tail arched up and away from the buttocks indicates excitement and anticipation, one clamped down hard between the buttocks means anger. Temper is also indicated by the tail being switched hard, normally from side to side.

Body attitude also helps tell us what state the horse is in. A normal, relaxed head carriage with relaxed tail means, not surprisingly, a relaxed horse. A tense, raised neck can mean excitement if the face looks excited and interested, and the tail, too, will be arched and steady. Some horses and ponies of Arab blood bring the tail up and over the quarters in extreme excitement.

Anger is expressed by an angry expression in the eye, the ears being pressed flat and hard back and down, the nostrils may be wrinkled up and back, and the teeth may grind in frustration, such as when a horse is being asked by a dominant rider to do something he does not like. Unfortunately, this grinding of teeth, accompanied by a switching tail, is not uncommonly seen in show-jumpers and dressage horses, less in other disciplines for some reason.

The ears being back can also mean a horse is trying his hardest at something, this is often seen in racehorses being pressed to the winning post, gymkhana ponies, event horses galloping to the finish, and so on.

If the ears are relaxed sideways, a bit floppy, it can mean the horse is very relaxed, perhaps dozing or sleeping, or not well. It can be difficult to differentiate between sleepiness and sickness, as in both the eyes may be

This horse is about to kick a dog who is closer to his heels than he likes. The rider should have been paying attention and either kept the dog away or turned the horse's heels away from the dog.

half closed or closed and the head down, or at least the neck horizontal instead of slightly raised, and the horse may be resting a hind leg. A guide is how long the horse has been like that. A dozing or sleeping horse will move after 15 to 30 minutes and perhaps potter about again or start eating, whereas a sick one may well spend most of his time in that pose.

A horse's intention to kick is shown, not surprisingly, by his lifting a hind foot in the air and perhaps waving it about a bit, probably aiming. His ears and at least one eye will be back towards the target, and he may look cross (nostrils up and back) or simply calmly calculating with a cold glint in his eye.

Fear is also shown with ears flat back, a frightened, wide-eyed look, skin seeming to be drawn tight across the face, the head usually high and tail flat. The muscles will be tense and hard.

A gesture often seen in young animals and not always understood because they do it to superior horses and humans, is submissive mouthing. The youngster snaps his lips and teeth open and shut with muzzle out-stretched towards the horse or human involved. This means: 'I'm young and harmless. Don't hurt me, I'm no threat to you.' If the youngster is hopeful of a kind reception his ears will possibly be forward, sideways if not sure, and probably back if a bit worried. Many novice people think that this mouthing means the animal is going to bite, but this is not so.

When a horse is thinking of biting, his muzzle may well be outstretched towards the horse or human

Submissive mouthing, shown here by a youngster snapping his mouth open and shut, is done by young animals to older ones and sometimes to humans.

This horse is clearly indicating his intention to bite some person or animal. His head is outstretched with mouth open and nostrils wrinkled up and back, and his ears are pressed hard, flat back.

concerned, his ears back, a nasty expression on his face and possibly the teeth bared or parted as he takes aim. Only young (usually two-year-olds and under) animals mouth, although the gesture is very occasionally seen in extremely submissive older animals and sometimes in mares to a stallion, again usually submissive or inexperienced mares. It has been seen in a young stallion to an elderly mare whom he was mating for his first time.

If a horse is feeling unwell, apart from being lethargic and standing or lying in an apparently dozing position for rather a long time, he will probably also have a hang-dog expression about him, maybe his eyes will look sunken, and he will almost certainly not want to bother with other horses. If he is in the field he will probably distance himself from them; in the stable he may spend a lot of time at the back of the box, although this can also be a sign of great stress and depression due to over-confinement, lack of exercise, freedom and other equine contact.

In lameness, horses often rest the lame leg. As they frequently rest with a hind leg resting and the hip on that side down a little, novices often feel unsure about this, but the horse's general attitude may help. If he looks uneasy and shifts his weight and the

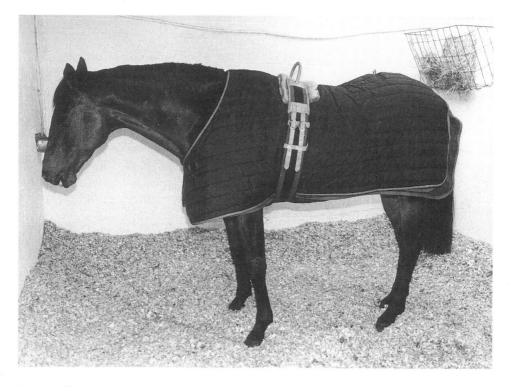

Every effort should be made to keep horses happy and content, by not over-stabling them and by giving them freedom and company as much as possible. Horses confined to stables for most of the time can exhibit all the classic signs of unhappiness – standing bored at the back of the box, looking dull and lethargic, grinding the teeth (a sign of stress) and showing little interest in life or in what is going on outside. It does not take much for so-called 'stable vices' to develop under these conditions – neuroses brought about by inappropriate management.

leg fairly often it is probably painful or uncomfortable and if he rests it backwards or forwards rather than next to its neighbour this can also indicate lameness. Horses never rest their forelegs, but stand with them together unless spreading them to reach down for something or wandering very slowly about their field grazing. If a horse stands resting a front leg, suspect trouble. He may rest it forwards or back, seeming to take the weight on heel or toe and may

shift his position and move the leg as if trying to relieve the discomfort.

Close attention to all these points should help you become fairly familiar with your horse's feelings. It should help you decide whether the horse is unwell and forewarn you when a horse is going to bite or kick.

With some experience and sensitivity, you will become quite adept at understanding your horse's language, and this can only improve your relationship with him.

INDEX

Numbers in *italic* refer to illustrations